TEACHERS CAN
MAKE A
DIFFERENCE

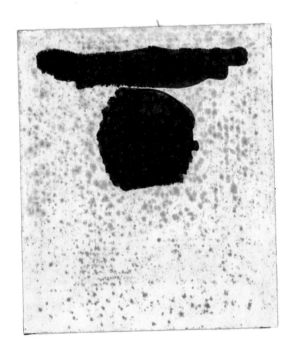

STUDIES OF THE PERSON

This Studies of the Person series was originally founded and developed by Carl R. Rogers and William R. Coulson, and is now under the managing editorship of William R. Coulson.

TEACHERS
CAN
MAKE A
DIFFERENCE

GERALD F. COREY

California State University,
Fullerton

CHARLES E. MERRILL PUBLISHING COMPANY
A Bell & Howell Company   Columbus, Ohio

In the memory of my father,
Dr. Joseph J. Corey

Published by

CHARLES E. MERRILL PUBLISHING COMPANY
A Bell & Howell Company
Columbus, Ohio

International Standard Book Number: 0-675-09001-6

Library of Congress Catalog Card Number: 72-92575

1 2 3 4 5 6 7 8 — 78 77 76 75 74 73

PRINTED IN THE UNITED STATES OF AMERICA

PREFACE

Why another book on teachers? The theme throughout these pages is that teachers can make a significant difference in the lives of the students they teach, and that the most valuable tool a teacher has to work with is himself. The message of this book is that teachers can become therapeutic people—people who are conducive to the growth of their students. Hopefully, this book should provide you with some areas that are crucially related to the human aspects of teaching and learning. My attempt is to help educators and future educators to examine their motivations for teaching, to focus upon the dimensions of the personhood of the teacher, to suggest ways of growth, and to provide some examples of teachers who are reaching students in ways that are unique to their own personalities.

You may sense a bias throughout the entire book—that the key to any significant change in education will rest with the teacher himself. Too often teachers act as though they were powerless. They complain endlessly about the system that hampers their creativity, but rarely do they look within themselves to discover the source of their real power. I suggest that the key to educational reformation can be found within the courage of each teacher to become that person that he is capable of becoming. He can affect significant change if he has self-awareness, and if he is willing to engage in risk-taking behavior. The central issues that will be explored in this book are:

- What does schooling do to the teacher? Do we teach the same way we were taught? Are educators able to transcend their own conditioning and break through to new levels?
- What are some of the psychological dynamics operating in the selection of teaching as a career? What are some healthy (and some not-so-healthy) reasons for staying in teaching? Why is it necessary to be aware of our needs and motivations if we are to affect positive change?
- What are the dimensions of the teacher as a therapeutic person? How is the teacher's struggle to become a person vitally related to becoming a positive force in the life of students?
- How can the encounter group be used as a vehicle for personal growth? What are the implications for such groups in teacher education? How do teachers perceive and evaluate their experience in these groups?
- How can we educate a new breed of teachers? Will traditional

v

teacher-education courses affect change in prospective teachers? What kind of teacher-education is needed?

- What are some examples of teachers who are making a difference with their students? What are these teachers like as people? How do they view their roles as teachers? What are their classrooms like, and how do they attain their objectives? What do their students say about them as teachers and persons, and how do these students feel about being in their class?
- Can school be changed? Can constructive change occur *within* the system? What are the major barriers to the reformation of our schools? Why are teachers threatened when there is a departure from traditional methods?
- What are some specific things a teacher *can do now* in working toward becoming a more humanistic teacher—one who is uniquely himself and one who encourages the development of the uniqueness of his students.

Before delving into these areas I have shared my own experiences as a learner to allow you to know more of me. Since I have a bias, I want you to be aware of the nature of this bias. My intention is to stimulate thought and discussion, to encourage you to do further reading in related areas, and most of all to goad you into doing something now to enhance the interpersonal aspects of teaching and learning. My concern is to demonstrate the need for educators to see the internal barriers to educational change—the barriers within their own personhood. If teachers can develop their own humanity and not be afraid of being people instead of disembodied roles, then I feel that change within our classrooms can become a reality.

I would like to acknowledge the support and encouragement I have received from people who have been very special to me: Reverend Peter Ciklic, my first professor in psychology who inspired me to continue in the field; Dr. Jane Warters, whose confidence in me helped me complete a doctoral program; Dr. William Lyon, at one time my psychotherapist, then my clinical supervisor during internship, and now both a friend and colleague who helped me to learn the value of taking risks; and Dr. Christopher Rubel, a friend and colleague, who taught me the value of being human in working with people. I am especially grateful to the four teachers who shared their thoughts and personal feelings about teaching in this book: Patricia Dunbridge, Dick Newton, Linda Schneider, and Richard Jacobs. I thank Susan Simpson for her typing assistance. And most of all, I appreciate the stimulation for growing provided by my wife, Marianne, during the past eight years.

Gerald F. Corey

Idyllwild, California

CONTENTS

1

My Experiences as a Learner

When I read a book addressed to "living life more fully," I immediately ask: what about the author? Who is he? What kind of experiences, struggles, goals, failures, successes has he had? Why is he *really* writing another book on the subject of man's relationship to himself and others? What significant forces have been in his life that are instrumental in the shaping of his values, ideas, feelings, perceptions—and his very being as a person? I am disillusioned when I put the book aside if the author is still a mystery to me. I feel that I have been cheated; that the writer may have shared a point of view, but I am still left wondering where the *person* of the writer is!

Not only do I feel I should share some of my personal and professional background with my readers, but I *want* to disclose some significant aspects of my past and present existence so that you will have a frame of reference for understanding (and challenging) what I say. I do write in a personal style; I hope to explain the background for this bias, not merely historically, but in sharing the meaning for *me* of my experiences.

ELEMENTARY SCHOOL YEARS

I spent nine years in a Catholic elementary school. Frankly, my earliest contacts with school bordered on the traumatic. I never recall particularly wanting to go to school, and my true feelings were a mixture of hate and fear. I particularly came to fear the authority of the nuns.

One of the worst of my elementary school years was in the fifth grade. I received "promotion doubtful" checks on my report card along with a generous sampling of *D*'s and *F*'s. Out of approximately forty pupils in the fifth grade class, I was the only one to fail the entire year. Next year I returned to the same class, with the same teacher, with little change in my performance. The nun almost failed me for a second time, but I suppose she grew tired of me also! This experience was painful. I felt very much alone—that I had let down the teacher, my parents, and myself, too. I was a lonely child during these years and kept pretty much to myself.

1

I recall being bored most of the time. We memorized the catechism, did all kinds of distasteful arithmetic exercises, learned the capitals of all the countries as well as the exports and imports, memorized historical events, and spent most of our time performing rote activities.

The upper elementary grades seemed to be an extension of my earlier years. What I really learned was that it is good to be obedient. We must respect authority. If you do "good" work you will be rewarded, and punishment is assigned for "poor" work. Religion is the most important subject. All other subjects should relate to God and the Church. Don't ask questions of "Why?"; simply accept what you are told. Anger, hate, sloth, laziness, etc. are "bad" feelings and you shouldn't feel these ways.

My elementary school experience meant to me that I must be obedient and a "good boy" or else I would pay the price! I was told repeatedly that I was not working up to my potential, and that I could "do better" if only I would "apply my mind" to my schoolwork. I tried by making all sorts of noble resolves, but somehow my good intentions rarely came to fruition.

MY HIGH SCHOOL DAYS

If these first nine years didn't finish me as a learner, the next four years in a Catholic boys' school surely did! I was barely admitted to the high school because of my poor grade records. When I told the elementary school principal that I was accepted at the school, her reply was "Heavens! They surely must be hard up for students!"

My first year was sheer hell. I had changed my pattern; and for the first time in my life, I was really trying to succeed. However, my inadequate background was still with me. I failed algebra even though I tried my utmost. I hated physical education and was constantly harassed for not participating properly. In my other subjects, I simply was not prepared to compete with a demanding college preparatory program. In many ways high school was an extension of grade school—so much emphasis was placed upon memorizing, giving correct answers, learning rote material, and making notebooks.

Nevertheless, I became the good student and was rewarded by consistently being on the honor roll during my last three years in high school. I did most of the things that were expected of good students. I learned to translate Latin to English and English to Latin. I diagrammed sentences, memorized parts of speech, memorized vocabulary words, and memorized long poems. I read my religion book carefully and gave back all the answers in the book. I dutifully wrote detailed outlines of chapters in our history book and answered all the questions at the end of each chapter. I followed all the rules in compiling endless notebooks for each subject.

My high school experiences confirmed a learning of my grade school days—that obedience, respect, and compliance are rewarded with approval, good grades, and honors. But I never learned how to really think. I never felt encouraged to form my own values or ideas. In fact, if I ever did initiate any of my own thoughts or feelings, I was abruptly reminded of my "place." The highest premium was placed upon acceptance of external authority, and our duty was to learn and practice these external teachings. I confess: I learned my lessons well.

MY COLLEGE EXPERIENCE

I chose to attend a Catholic college for men run by the Jesuits, Loyola University at Los Angeles. During my five-year stay, I earned a bachelor's degree in psychology and a secondary teaching credential. I also earned a master's degree in educational psychology.

When I entered my freshman year at college, I knew I wanted to teach classes dealing in personal problems of young people. I'm sure my motivation was largely based upon my own experiences of pain during this period. During this year I took General Psychology and became "turned on" to this field. I found a teacher that cared in my psychology professor, Reverend Peter Ciklic. Father Ciklic was a dynamic and interesting lecturer who opened many new doors for me. I studied diligently and became one of his "best" students. I took every course he offered and enjoyed each experience immensely. He encouraged me to go to graduate school and get a doctorate in psychology. His confidence in me and our relationship stimulated my desire to become a psychologist.

My college years were "successful" in many respects. I earned a music scholarship to the college, found great satisfaction in being in the band, and earned high grades every year. I devoted myself fully to my studies, music, and preparing to become a teacher. But aside from these activities, I did not experience much of life during my college years.

In many respects, though, my college experiences reinforced what I had learned during my first thirteen years of schooling. I had simply decided to play the academic game and be rewarded. While I did take some exciting courses and meet some challenging professors, much of the experience was a repeat of high school. My main objection to my undergraduate education is that it was too narrow. There was no challenge of opposing viewpoints. Diversity of thinking was not encouraged. Instead, my task was to learn the truth, and then give back on examinations what I had heard in lecture and read in books.

MY GRADUATE SCHOOL EXPERIENCES

At the same time that I began teaching full-time in a public high school, I enrolled in the University of Southern California on a part-time basis. Five years later I earned a doctorate in counseling psychology and educational psychology; in the meantime I had acquired credentials in school counseling and school psychology.

Dr. Jane Warters, one of my professors at U.S.C., was a real source of encouragement to continue in the doctoral program when the future appeared very bleak to me. I felt blocked by two factors: my low math scores on the Graduate Record Examination and the required courses in elementary and advanced statistical methods. I just couldn't see how I could ever pass an advance statistics course when I had failed high school algebra and when I still had great difficulty in doing fractions. Dr. Warters assured me that I could get an elementary math book and tutor myself. She had far more faith in me than I did. I took her advice, and the statistics courses. This experience taught me that when a goal is important to a person, he can overcome obstacles to acquire learning that seems personally meaningful. It also taught me the value of support from a caring teacher.

In assessing my graduate school experience, my central complaint is that much of the work involved consisted in jumping over a variety of hurdles, including Graduate Record Examinations, comprehensive exams, qualifying exams, oral exams, seventy-six units of required courses, dissertation, and oral exam on dissertation. There was too much emphasis upon meeting external requirements, and too little attention directed at helping the doctoral candidate come to terms with defining his own responsibility for becoming an independent learner.

EXPERIENCES IN MY PERSONAL AND PROFESSIONAL LIFE

The past eleven years have been exciting, rewarding, and marked by some real changes for me, both professionally and personally. If I could summarize the one major learning over this period it would be that *the degree to which I can be effective as a helping person is determined by the degree to which I have become a person myself.* Briefly, let me describe the evolution of my professional career, and what I have learned from these experiences.

My first four years were spent as a teacher of psychology, English, and history at Whittier High School. In retrospect, these years were devoted almost exclusively to teaching and my graduate work. I began teaching in an authoritarian style and viewed homework, tests, and grades as almost sacred. This experience taught me that high school students need and want more than they receive from conventional teaching. Unfortunately, my early years of teaching were in a large part an imitation of the way I was taught. I was extremely enthused about my work, and I did make real efforts to give my students something more than I experienced in my schooling. In spite of my rigidity, I feel that my students tolerated my limitations because they sensed my enthusiasm, and they knew that I cared about teaching.

While I was a teacher of Senior English, a German exchange student was placed in my class. Marianne Schneider was an attractive, charming, bright, open person who had dared to come to America without knowing how to speak English. Marianne was a very significant person in my life who made me aware that the narrow preoccupation with school is not the totality of life. Ten minutes after she graduated, I asked her for a date; and two years later we went to Germany to be married.

During my first year as a teacher, I became involved in my own individual psychotherapy. This proved to be a major turning point in my life. As I mentioned earlier, most of my adult life has been synonymous with being a teacher. My life was comfortable, secure, narrow, and dull. Dr. William Lyon, a clinical psychologist, helped me to upset the narrowness of my limited world and encouraged me to open doors which I had kept sealed because of fear. For several years, Dr. Lyon was a significant instrument for me in discovering power within me and the ways I denied my power as a person. My experience in individual and group therapy opened doors that would surely have remained closed in my life. In essence, my encounters in psychotherapy gave me an awareness of what a tiny fraction of my human potential was being used. I became aware of the influences that my past experiences had upon me now. Since the beginning of my therapy, there have been periods of awakening, of struggle and conflict, of choice and decision, of wrestling with the meaning and responsibilities of personal freedom, and of experimenting with more enriching ways of being. There have also been the periods of stagnation, of accepting contentment and refusing growth, and of being closed to new learning. The periods I especially value are the times when I dared taken a risk. Generally, I have found that most of the risks I have taken have been well worth the gamble.

For two years I was an instructor in psychology at Rio Hondo Junior College in Whittier. I functioned mainly as a lecturer. What I learned from this experience was that I eventually become bored with hearing my lectures, even though I don't rigidly adhere to notes. Even though I was apparently able to have an attentive and interested audience, I felt something was missing. It was my show, and the students were the passive members of the audience. The experience also showed me that there is more to learning than telling, and that the student is cheated if he is merely the passive receptacle of learning.

I then left teaching for a year and worked as a counseling psychologist in the Counseling Center at California State Polytechnic University in Pomona; I initiated a part-time private practice in psychotherapy and did my internship as a psychotherapist at the same time. This was a depressing, discouraging, difficult year. I had feelings of inadequacy as a therapist, for the results of my labor were slow to be realized. I was *most* impatient, and I'm sure I projected my feeling of incompetency to my clients, almost as if I were telling them, "Damn it! Hurry up and get rid of your symptoms! Don't stay troubled for long—get cured quickly. Let me know that I am effective!" At this time I returned for more individual therapy to deal with areas of my life that I was reluctant to face before I encountered some of these struggles in my clients. I learned a lesson—that a therapist (or any member of the "helping" professions) is not able to assist a client in facing or resolving any issue that the therapist himself has refused to work out. It was then that I acquired another significant learning: all of my professional training, my entire academic background, my degrees and credentials and licenses, don't really count a damn when it came to face-to-face encounters with a person wrestling with his internal conflicts. External signs (degrees and credentials) simply are not where it's at. Instead, all I can rely upon is my own being—how far I have matured and effectively dealt with the unfinished business that resides in me. Gradually I learned that I cannot help a client cope with his depression if I have been busily engaged in running from my own depression. If I have not opened myself to my own feelings of anger, jealousy, sexuality, and dependency, I cannot be an instrument for another in facing these feelings. If I have arranged my life in a protected style, I cannot possibly understand the desperation of the suicidal client who presents me with his hopelessness. Can I assist another to find greater meaning in his life, if I have avoided coming to terms with my own emptiness? How authentic is my invitation to a client to become transparent through self-disclosure if he perceives me as hiding behind a professional facade? Painfully, I learned these lessons—and I'm still struggling with many of these same questions.

In the time since my internship I have learned how much I owe to my friend and colleague, Dr. Christopher Rubel. I was an associate of Dr. Rubel's in a part-time private practice as a psychologist. He demonstrated the value of a therapist's authenticity, and from Dr. Rubel I learned that clients respond to the human dimension they experience in their therapist. These years in being a therapist have confirmed my hunch that it is important for a helping person to function as a model. A counselor must be working toward the kind of wholeness in his own life that he encourages in his client's development. Those who come to us for counseling surely ought to ask "What has your own counseling done for you in life? What kind of person are you?" One of the main things I have learned from my experience as a psychotherapist is that there are no sharp distinctions between "therapist" and "client"; and that my being as natural and spontaneous as I can be seems to be contagious.

For four years I was associated with the Teacher Preparation Center at California State Polytechnic University in Pomona. Many of the details of my work there are described in Chapter 5 and Chapter 7. I feel that I probably did more personal changing in these four years than I did in the first thirty years totalled. I'm sure this change is reflected in my teaching. I have learned to trust my students more, to give them more responsibility for their own learning, and to share more of myself with them. I'm finding that the more I am able to trust myself, the more I'm able to trust students.

I am now in a new position as an associate professor of interdisciplinary and special studies at California State University at Fullerton. My central functions are to teach courses in the human services program, to develop innovative courses, to train people in becoming group counselors, and to "teach" a variety of self-development and self-awareness courses. I am excited by this move, and I find myself wondering what it will mean in the next few years.

CONCLUDING COMMENTS

This book is the result of my experiences as a learner and teacher. In addition to teaching educational psychology courses for prospective teachers, I have taught a variety of inservice workshop courses, from which I have become more aware of both the personal and professional problems of teachers. Without this experience I doubt that I would have attempted to write this book.

After reading about the extent of my professional life, you might be wondering what I have left for my personal life and for my family. I admit that, for me, there is a danger of becoming so involved in my

professional projects that much of my energy is channeled in this direction. I do wrestle with this tendency to become overly invested with work; and I do value free time, time with my family, and time alone. My wife has been the most significant change agent in my life. She is very involved in the same kind of work as I am, and she is currently in training as a psychological counselor. We have been good for each other in the sense that we have encouraged each other to try undertakings we thought impossible. I'm aware that it is not easy to live with a psychologist, and I truly feel fortunate in finding a woman that cannot only tolerate, but enjoy, living with me. Our two preschool daughters, Heidi and Cindy, have taught me that it is worth it to love. They remind me of the delights of being a child, and I envy their capacity for being spontaneous, for experiencing all feelings, and being blunt and honest. I decided awhile back that it is very important for me to be a father, and that I want to know my kids and let them know me. We have a mountain house in Idyllwild where we spend much of our free time as a family, and this mountain retreat is essential for me in keeping my own integrity. I learned earlier that I must become sensitive to my own limitations and sense when I have a need for detachment from people. When I am insensitive to this need, I experience myself like a computer and others see me as becoming more formal, detached, and impersonal.

ORGANIZATION OF THE REMAINDER OF THE BOOK

This book is my attempt to share various aspects of my experiences in education and teacher training. Each of the following chapters are topics to which I have given considerable thought; they are separate aspects of my experience in consulting, teaching, conducting workshops, and working with public school teachers and students. Each topic deals with the central theme of how teachers make a difference in the lives of their students, and each chapter is an attempt to expand upon the importance of the teacher knowing himself, and communicating this self to his students. This is a plea for more personal teaching.

The next chapter is a critical appraisal of the effects of traditional education upon the learner. I attempt to clarify the ways in which teachers form their concepts about the role of the teacher, the place of the student, the nature of learning, and the outcomes of our schooling upon our personality. This chapter is based upon not only my own experiences, but also upon my observations of high school and college students and teacher interns.

Chapter 3 examines some crucial questions: Why do people become teachers? What personal needs motivate the selection of teaching as a vocation? How can teachers become therapeutic persons? What are some of the characteristics of teachers who are making a difference?

Following is a chapter that explores the nature of teachers' struggles in becoming therapeutic persons. Here the dimensions of the teacher as a person are described. While no formula is presented, the aim of the chapter is to stimulate your thinking to look at yourself and discover ways of extending your influence as a teacher by developing yourself as a person.

The next chapter is a follow-up where the encounter group is described as one way of helping teachers grow personally. The personal growth group is one avenue teachers can explore in their search for improving their capacity to look at themselves and to learn to use their personhood as an instrument in their teaching. The encounter group is described in large part through the eyes of teachers who participated in these groups, and they explain how the group experience affected them in their personal and professional lives.

Chapter 6 describes my approach in teacher education. Some ideas are presented to suggest alternative ways of educating more humanistically oriented teachers.

In the next chapter, you are introduced to four teachers through personal interviews in which they share some of their beliefs about teaching, learning, students, and ways of changing education. Then you can see these teachers through the eyes of their students. These teachers are examples of persons who are struggling to become more effective in their work, and they are effecting significant differences.

Chapter 8 deals with the challenge of reforming our schools along humanistic lines. An experiment—an attempt to develop a "school within a school"—is described, and attitudes of teachers toward this type of change are examined. Here the issue is how we can change the attitudes of established teachers who are frequently theatened by change. How can teachers be encouraged to develop more openness to alternative approaches?

When you finish the book I hope you will say: "So what does this mean to me? How do the ideas in this book apply to me, and what can I do now? Where can I go from here?" The final chapter is designed not to produce a list of ready-made answers, but to present some guidelines and suggest directions for you to begin NOW. My hope is to stimulate your own thought on how you can reach more of your students. An annotated reading list provides an excellent beginning in working toward the goal of becoming the teacher who *can* make a difference.

Before continuing with the remainder of this book, I suggest you refer to "Twenty Questions," pages 182–85. If you examine these questions before reading the book, they may serve to put into focus the central ideas in the following chapters. Then, after you finish the book, I recommend that you review the questions and see how you respond to each of them. Whatever you do, I hope you'll enjoy your reading.

2

What Schooling Does to Teachers

I have found that reliving my memories as a learner has been extremely helpful in deciding which ways I would like to change my teaching. Throughout my school experiences there were certain messages transmitted to me, and most of these did not assist me in becoming an active learner. I find that the graduate students with whom I work who are preparing to become teachers have also learned definite lessons. This chapter examines the effects of schooling upon the ways we perceive our role as a teacher.

In this chapter I frequently use "we" with a distinct purpose. I still wrestle with my past influencing my present teaching behavior. When I began teaching I taught in an authoritarian manner. There are still parts of the "old me" in the "present me," and I need to struggle to remain open to ways that I tend to become rigid. In my present teaching there is structure; I do have some definite expectations of students, I do have some minimum requirements, and I do not feel comfortable in granting total freedom to my students to do whatever they choose. Where I really struggle is in deciding *how much* freedom to grant to my students, and how much responsibility I need to assume for their learning. There are many times that I am guilty of some of the errors I write about in this chapter, but I can say that I attempt to remain open to my teaching style and the effects it has upon my students.

Those of us who are "successful" as students often become teachers. By "successful" I mean that we have learned to play academic games well. From our early school years we learn certain success strategies based upon conformity. For this conformity to what our teachers and school establishment expect, we are rewarded with rich doses of teacher praise, honors, and good grades. *Unless we become aware of what our schooling has done to us as learners, most probably we will teach in the same style in which we were taught—and with sometimes disastrous results to the learners in our classrooms.* Let me outline some of the subtle messages that are communicated to us from kindergarten through graduate school. In compiling this list, I'm quite sure many readers will react negatively, feeling that I am painting a dismal picture of education. Many will protest, saying "But my learning years were different, and I can remember only wonderful experiences." In my work in teacher preparation, I have come to realize that what I am about to describe is unfortunately typical for the majority of teacher candidates.

MESSAGES TRANSMITTED TO US AS LEARNERS

PLEASE THE TEACHER

From our earliest contact with teachers we soon learn the urgency of pleasing the teacher. College students unconsciously develop this strategy of quickly assessing what the professor wants, and they give him back on exams what he feeds them during lectures without questioning him. It's sad to hear graduate students exchanging anxieties before a class—"What does he want us to do and say?" The saddest note is that many individuals who are prepared to become teachers rarely are aware of the dynamics of these academic games.

Basically, then, we discover that the important thing is to please our own teachers; and if they are pleased with us, then we "gain" the "rewards" of recognition, praise, high grades, honors, and gold stars. The desire to please our selves becomes relatively unimportant. As we continue this search to please others, we gradually lose touch with our own internal compasses. Our radar sets are finely tuned to picking up external cues, but the internal cues become dulled.

What is the impact of this need to please others upon our role as teachers? I suspect that most teachers perpetuate this same kind of outer orientation with their students. We tend to reinforce behavior that is in accord with these standards and goals, and ignore or punish behavior that does not seem consistent with these standards. So, often without ever verbalizing it, we might be saying to our students, "What you think or feel is relatively unimportant; find out what I expect, and be sure and make me feel good by giving me what I expect."

NEVER QUESTION THE TEACHER'S AUTHORITY

In our schooling experiences we learn that a teacher is an authority figure and we ought not even to question this authority. Obedience is taught as a prime virtue. What the teacher utters is truth, and who is a lowly student to question this truth? As we progress through each grade level, we often become indoctrinated with the idea that teachers possess the gift of infallibility.

The implications of this early learning are vast for our role as teachers. A common anxiety voiced by student-teachers is: "What will I do, or how will I feel, if a student asks me a question that I can't answer? Or what if my students discover that I make some mistakes during a lesson?"

LEARNING IS THE RESULT OF EXTERNAL MOTIVATION

Watch infants and small children eagerly work at new tasks simply for the intrinsic pleasure of making new discoveries. They are motivated by the sheer joy of learning itself. If only we could allow our children to continue this kind of intrinsic search and research, both learning and life itself could be more ecstatic than the drudgery that it often is. George Leonard's book *Education and Ecstasy* (14) * is devoted to this theme. He indicates that we have all the basic know-how to allow for joyful learning *now*, but our encrusted notions of what education should be prevents it from becoming personally enriching.

John Holt, in *How Children Learn* (7), makes essentially the same point. Children *do* learn, because it is a basic human need and because it is fun. Curiosity, exploration, the need to manipulate, the need to discover how things work, are parts of the growth of healthy children. Competition, threats, and external motivation are not needed to entice the unschooled. Children will endure frustration and failure and still persist in their attempts to find solutions to problems which are personally meaningful.

What happens to these intrinsically oriented learners? What does schooling do to us? Unfortunately most of us have been sold the idea that without external goading no learning will occur. This idea is demonstrated in a number of ways: by dividing the class into groups, and encouraging competition among these groups; by emphasizing external rewards such as grades, gold stars, praise, smiling faces; by pitting one student against another. As teachers, we develop all sorts of strategies based upon external motivation for behavior. These strategies indirectly foster a learning which is oriented toward winning as opposed to the kind of learning that occurs because of its own sake.

Physical education departments are notorious for perpetuating this myth that learning ought to be based upon external motivation. Recently I was at a high school faculty conference where several depart-

---

* Numbers in parentheses refer to the annotated reading list found on pages 187–99.

ments were attempting to substitute a pass–fail type of grading system for the *A* through *F* system. Without even hearing the proposal, a coach, also the head of the P. E. Department, angrily spoke out: "I'm opposed to this. The trouble with our country today is that our standards are becoming lax, and by going to a pass–fail system, students are bound to goof off. Take away the pressure of grades, and you take away all incentive for learning! No, I say we need grades to motivate our kids!"

I'm very impatient with this philosophy. It's based upon a view of man which I simply cannot accept. The philosophy assumes that learning is equated with drudgery, that school needs to be a chore, and that learning can occur only with guidance from experts along with continual urging by these experts. To me, a competition with self is far healthier. Why can we not allow learners to work toward the goal of bettering their own standards and working toward personal excellence? I'm convinced that this is far from idealism; it can be a reality, if only we as teachers modify our basic attitudes that we acquired uncritically in our early experiences as students.

RIGHT-ANSWER SYNDROME

One of the most pervasive myths that we acquire with our formal schooling is that there are "right answers" to every problem. An extension is that if we are to survive in the academic race, we damn well ought to learn these right answers. We come to expect that there are solutions to all problems that are posed.

The destructive aspect of this right-answer syndrome is found in our search outside of ourselves for these solutions. In a real way we learn to distrust our own judgment, feeling, and sense of direction. We become afraid of risking. Experimentation and trial-and-error behavior in our learning become rarer. Before we take a chance, we need to know that we will come up with the "correct answer," which is, of course, the answer our teacher expects. Since acceptance of the teacher's values is prized, we often become uncritical in our acceptance of the values of our mentors. We become more expert in learning the rules of the game-playing structure we call education. In learning to succeed at this game, we of necessity relinquish coming to grips with our own values. Instead, we substitute external standards for our own. The tragedy is that before long, we are no longer capable of discrimination between *our* values and *other's* values that have been superimposed upon us. They become one and the same. We become what others expect us to become.

In *How Children Fail* (6) Holt gives a penetrating analysis of the effects upon learners of this right-answer orientation. His position is *most children in school fail.* They fail because they are afraid, bored, and confused. Holt describes the "really able thinkers" as those who do not feel the strong need to please adults, but please themselves. Most children fear failure, are afraid of being called stupid, and are afraid of risking behavior where they might feel stupid. It is this fear that inhibits authentic learning. As Holt says, "The scared learner is always a poor learner" (p. 167). We destroy the learner's curiosity for learning by making him be afraid to gamble, fear making mistakes, seek to please others, seek the approval of others, work for external rewards, be afraid to experiment or explore the unknown, not trust his own common sense and judgment, and be bored with meaningless tasks.

When we finally receive our hard-earned teaching credentials, and we find ourselves now on the other side of the teacher's desk, we unconsciously (sometimes even consciously) perpetuate this error of correct answers for every problem. We become rigid in expecting our students to spout back the answer we have in mind, to give the correct interpretation of a poem, to arrive at the single and unambiguous right answer to questions dealing with facts, judgment, values, or attitudes. Because of our conditioning as learners, we encourage convergent thinking—thought processes that terminate in a narrow answer.

This kind of thinking is built upon the premise that learning is a closed system. Questions are raised, and there are always appropriate answers to be found. It stifles creativity, it prevents further inquiry, it ceases the process of self-initiated learning, and it discourages us from entering the arena of unknown territory. Divergent thinking —or thought processes involving a number of alternative answers—is based upon a radically different model of teaching–learning. It assumes the possibility of flexibility, of many avenues to truth, and of many desirable approaches to problem solving. It fosters creativity. Learning becomes an open system where questions lead to further questions. The sad thing is that most teachers who have been educationally reared with a closed system of learning find it intolerable to experience the kind of ambiguity that is necessarily a part of divergent–creative thinking. Instead of confronting our own anxiety, we may cling to the right-answer orientation we experienced and force this pattern on our own students.

If we become aware of our conditioning, as I have been describing, then we can transcend this conditioning and provide a more fruitful kind of learning process for our own students. I don't see anyone as condemned to teach the way he was taught. As a prerequisite for change, it is essential that the teacher become conscious of the effects that his education has had upon him as learners. Then, if he is disgusted enough, angry enough, frustrated enough, and hungry enough to create a different kind of learning environment for his students, there is hope for change.

In *Education and Ecstasy,* an exciting book on the future possibilities of what education could become, Leonard says,

> Right answers, specialization, standardization, narrow competition, eager acquisition, aggression, detachment from the self. Without them, it has seemed, the social machinery would break down. Do not call the schools cruel or unnatural for furthering what society has demanded. The reason we now need radical reform in education is that society's demands are changing radically. It is quite safe to say that the human characteristics now being inculcated will not work much longer. Already they are not only inappropriate, but destructive. If education continues along the old track, humanity will sooner or later simply destroy itself (14, pp. 124–25).

LEARNERS SHOULD BE PASSIVE

Another message of formal schooling is the idea that passive acceptance is more desirable than active criticism and self-initiated learning. In a very real way many of us have been molded into a passive stance. Our business as students is to answer questions put to us by teachers, not to engage actively in critical thinking. Surely we were out of place if we dared to query: "Why are we doing what we are doing?" "Whose facts are these?" "What does this work mean to me?" "Are there other ways of viewing this problem besides the teacher's view or the textbook's view?" We acquire a passive, receptive, reactive style. If we dare to assume an active style, chances are we are put down and quickly instructed on our role as students.

In my work with graduate-level students preparing to become teachers, I painfully experience the effects of this passive orientation on their spirits as learners. Even as graduate students who will soon be teaching, they seem lost and uncertain when they are asked to reach into themselves and express what they think or feel about issues related to their future profession. It is as though they have no thoughts, no opinions, no feelings, or no substantial views of their own. Some will sit passively in a seminar group for an entire quarter; and even when they are confronted with their passivity as learners, they utter: "I'm not used to a class where you are expected to share your own views. I've felt that I've always had to listen and accept what was being taught." In discussing this concern with my classes, I find that they, too, are afraid to risk venturing their own ideas. They prefer to play it safe, and become "good listeners," only rarely making any verbal contributions. Even by eliminating tests and examinations, substituting exciting paperback books for a dry textbook, and guaranteeing a blanket *B* grade for the course, this situation is not radically altered. The damage done to them before they became graduate students is too pervasive to be undone in a single quarter.

The question that I pose for teachers-to-be is this: If you are basically a passive learner, then how can you possibly allow your own students to become actively engaged in initiating and directing their own learning? Here is another example of how we tend to perpetuate our own learning styles upon the children we teach.

So what should teachers do? First, recognize where we are ourselves on the spectrum of passive–active learning. This is a beginning. From here we can risk assuming more personal responsibility for our own learning. Eventually, if we can become more active ourselves, we can encourage our students to become more analytical, more critical as learners, and far more involved personally in the nature and direction of their own learning. Some excellent reflection material can be found in Postman and Weingartner's book *Teaching as a Subversive Activity* (15). The authors suggest that teachers ought to work toward a new education that would set out to cultivate students who were experts at "crap detecting." Teachers should teach students how to be "subversive" by encouraging their students to ask "What is it good for?" Instead of being in the "information dissemination" business, teachers ought to allow and encourage students to go beyond what others tell them and to ask substantive questions. Postman and Weingartner make a key point: "Once you have learned to ask questions—relevant and appropriate and substantial questions—you have learned how to learn and no one can keep you from learning whatever you want to or need to know" (p. 23).

LEARNING: A PRODUCT

I suspect that the majority of us were product-oriented instead of process-oriented. Our conditioning made us interested in obtaining the answer. As Holt indicated in *How Children Fail* (6), our schools produce children who are answer-centered, not problem-centered; because schools worship right answers, teachers themselves are answer-centered, and teachers are not aware of the distinction between product and process orientation.

If we as teachers could only shift this focus to creating a climate where students could find excitement in the *process* of learning itself, what a joy learning would become. Just learning the process itself of how to paint, play a musical instrument, or water ski is rewarding. When we achieve the end (product), we often search for new things to master. Why is it so difficult for teachers to grasp this concept of the value of the inquiry and exploration itself? Instead of teaching the *what* of learning, teachers ought to be concerned with the *how* of learning. When children learn how to learn, they become their own teachers. Perhaps this is the clue to why so many teachers devote most of their energies to "teaching" children—teaching them the what. This is the way they make students depend upon them. They can become the superior guru who has all the wisdom, and their function becomes one of pouring knowledge into the empty heads of uninitiated and uninformed students, who in turn, can stand in awe of the teacher's magnificent brilliance. Think of it—if we set them free of us, then they might not need us any more. This thought is too frightening for many teachers to contemplate seriously.

If you're interested in a more complete discussion of a process orientation to education utilizing the inquiry method, I recommend two fine books: William Glasser's *School Without Failure* (13) and Postman and Weingartner's *Teaching as a Subversive Activity* (15). In the latter book, the authors indicate that the inquiry method stresses learning as a process, not as a product, in which the learner is active and involved in the search himself. In response to the question of what good learners believe and do, a summary of their comments includes (15, p. 31):

1. Good learners have confidence in their ability to learn.
2. Good learners enjoy solving problems and learning.
3. Good learners know what is relevant to their survival and what is not.
4. Good learners prefer to rely on their own judgment.
5. Good learners are not fearful of being wrong.
6. Good learners are not fast answerers.
7. Good learners are flexible.
8. Good learners know how to ask meaningful questions.
9. Good learners examine their own assumptions.
10. Good learners continually verify what they believe.
11. Good learners do not need to have a final and absolute answer for every problem.

But as Postman and Weingartner claim, there can be no significant innovation in education that does not have as its center the attitudes of teachers. The beliefs and assumptions of teachers *are* the learning atmosphere, and teachers determine the quality of life within it. They list the attitudes of the inquiry teacher which are reflected in his behavior as:*

1. The teacher rarely tells students what he thinks they ought to know.
2. His basic mode of discourse with students is questioning (uses both convergent and *divergent* questions!).
3. He does not accept a single statement or one right answer to a question, for right answers serve to terminate thought.
4. He encourages student–student interaction and avoids acting as judge of the quality of the ideas presented.
5. He rarely summarizes the positions taken by students.
6. His lessons develop from the responses of students and not from a previously determined "logical" structure.
7. His lessons propose a problem for students.
8. He measures his success in terms of *behavioral changes* in students (15, p. 34).

SCHOOL LEARNING IS SEPARATE FROM LIVING

As I review my experience in schools, I am aware that indirectly a message was communicated that what goes on inside a classroom has very little relevance for outside living. A typical criticism heard by learners on all levels is that school learning is divorced from "real life." School is a place where we perform meaningless tasks toward meaningless goals. Much of our learning is apparent learning which consists of learning what others expect of us. Authentic learning, the kind where understanding occurs and where there is an integration of our intellect and feelings, is not common in school.

I ask you to ask yourself: "How much of my school learning has been simply apparent learning?" "How many classes stressed only the outcomes of apparent learning?" "What are some obstacles to genuine learning in my own experience as a student?" Attempt to cite specific examples of barriers to meaningful learning. As we know, examinations do not measure the degree of learning which is personally significant. They assess only the peripheral knowledge we have amassed and serve as an index to how well we have accomplished tasks set for us by others.

---

* From *Teaching as a Subversive Activity* by Neil Postman and Charles Weingartner. Copyright © 1969 by Neil Postman and Charles Weingartner. Reprinted by permission of the publisher, Delacorte Press.

Real learning occurs when we can relate and apply knowledge to specific problems. When we are immersed in any learning activity which has personal value, we learn quickly and efficiently. Each of you can give your own examples to validate this concept of personal involvement in learning. When I was in high school and college, I was required to "go through" four years of Spanish. Now I can barely say "adios" in Spanish. However, by contrast, before I married my wife, I visited Germany to meet her relatives. I secured an elementary German book and taught myself more German in a few weeks than I learned in Spanish with four years of required instruction.

On this point of rate of learning, Leonard feels that *every* child can learn to read, write, spell, to manipulate quantities, to learn all the hard stuff of present-day schooling, in less than one-third of the time it now takes. Leonard's position is that schools are geared to halt learning. He states:

> Perhaps half of all learning ability was squelched in the earliest elementary grades, where children found out that there exist predetermined and unyielding "right answers" for everything, that following instructions is what really counts and, that the whole business of education is mostly dull and painful (14, p. 120).

THE SELF IS IGNORED IN EDUCATION

What can be more vitally related to education than a consideration of the self of the learner? An education that dismisses or does not recognize the importance of the goals, perceptions, values, feelings, and dreams of the learner can be only sterile and fragmented. Yet from my observations of elementary and secondary classrooms, that is what is most frequently denied. Learning about peripheral topics such as imports and exports of a country, facts about historical events, parts of speech, mathematical exercises, and scientific formulas is emphasized far more than learning about one's self.

In the backgrounds of most teachers few can cite courses that dealt with issues such as: What do I want from life? What are my basic values and how did I obtain them? What kind of person am I capable of becoming? What am I becoming? What am I doing now to obtain my life goals? What is the meaning of life? How can I become more aware of my potentialities as a person? What is worth striving for? Who am I? What is my destiny? What are some of the values I choose to live for? What is worth dying for? How do I perceive the world? What do I want to accomplish with my life? Take away the consideration of these issues in education, and we also take the guts out of learning.

If we concentrate merely on the peripheral aspects, we are left with meaningless abstractions, bits of unrelated data, useless knowledge, sterile theories. I fear that the bulk of our education as teachers could be characterized by denial of the self of the learner and concentration on topics distantly related to our lives.

Speaking on the denial of self in education, Clark Moustakas, in his book *Personal Growth*, states:

> He is denied: as a self, he simply does not exist. His own feelings, perceptions, interests, senses, his own spontaneous directions are ignored. He is no longer an active force participating in the shape and destiny of his life and involved and committed so that his diversity of expression becomes indigenous to the real growth of his self. He is not free; he has no genuine choice and he is not responsible in any meaningful sense of the term (86, p. 7).

If learning is to be more than isolated bits and pieces of nonmeaningful information stored in the learner's head, then it is essential that students are challenged by real issues. We need to engage the learner with concerns that have personal meaning in his life space. And this can be done without ignoring the mastery of basic fundamentals needed for understanding and application. Dr. George Brown and his associates at the University of California at Santa Barbara have worked for several years at developing humanistic approaches to the teaching–learning process. Their goal is not to discard the conventional curriculum in public schools, but rather to train teachers with a philosophy based upon integrating the central concerns of the student with the subject matter to be learned. In his book, *Human Teaching for Human Learning* (20), Brown describes his work in training teachers in developing their own techniques for applying the conventional curriculum to the lives of the learner. The emphasis is not solely upon the feelings of the learner, but on an integration of the cognitive and the affective aspects. Knowledge is acquired in a way that has reference to the feelings, ambitions, goals, values, attitudes, and life space of the learner. Unfortunately, education has focused almost exclusively upon the cognitive domain (development of the "mind"), while the affective domain (development of the feelings and values) has received little attention. A goal of humanistic education is to develop the whole self of the learner, both his mind and heart, rather than fracture the individual as most traditional education does.

Yet this myth that learning can occur without a relationship to the concerns of the learner is still pervasive in schools. We continue to force students to "learn" a multitude of subjects that we, with our advanced experience and know-how and wisdom, deem essential to their well-being. We assume that we know what's best for them, and that because of their intellectual and emotional immaturity we owe it to them to dictate what they need to learn in order to "adjust" and to become productive and successful citizens. Perhaps we can coerce them to be physically present in the classroom where they are "taught" required subjects, but even the most traditional teacher will agree that it is impossible for learning to occur unless the learner is motivated. The problem with many teachers is their assumption that motivation cannot emerge from within the learner, which leads them to develop all sorts of tricks so that the learner will learn what is "good" for him.

LEARNERS ARE OBJECTS, NOT PERSONS

Related to the discussion of the exclusion of self from education is the viewing of children and youth as objects, not as persons. We label students "accelerated," "culturally deprived," "unmotivated," "behavior disordered," "mentally retarded," "average," and a host of other catchy titles. While labels are convenient for us, they often cause us to view the students we teach as objects.

There are a multitude of ways in which teachers depersonalize students. You might examine what you see as your central function as a teacher. In *Teaching as a Subversive Activity*, Postman and Weingartner describe five types of teachers that surely relate to their students as nonpersons (15, p. 82):

1. "The Lamplighter"—illuminates minds.
2. "The Gardener"—cultivates minds, plants seeds, and helps plants grow.
3. "The Personnel Manager"—keeps student's minds busy.
4. "The Muscle Builder"—strengthens flabby minds.
5. "The Bucket Filler"—fills up empty minds.

Too often adults see children as unfinished creatures, as objects to be molded, shaped, directed, and manipulated in many ways. As Moustakas observes in *Personal Growth*, when adults consistently treat a child as an object, he soon begins to react as a thing and as a nonperson:

> When a child is perceived as an empty vessel to be filled with facts and explanations, there is a real danger that he will lose touch with his own awareness and response to life. . . . In such a setting, learning is divorced from human values; the people in the school are alienated from each other and from themselves. The child engages

in activities that have nothing to do with his own integrity, with his own responses to life. He is alienated from his teacher, who does not exist as a person, who does not recognize his uniqueness, and who does not know that reality is based on personal perceptions and commitments to life, not on external purpose, motive, goal, and authority (86, p. 42).

I encourage you to examine honestly to what degree you have become an object as a result of your own schooling. Consider the implications of being treated as a thing, instead of being viewed as a responsible person with goals and unique potentiality. If we have become depersonalized, alienated from ourselves, others and the world, then what are we able to bring of ourselves that is real into our classrooms? If we have been treated as objects, manipulated according to the whims of those who taught us, told what to think, and how to think, have we not lost our sense of being as a person? Will we not relate to our students as things also? Will our relationships be characterized by It–It interactions in place of I–Thou human encounters? I raise these questions as challenges, hoping each reader will spend time in becoming aware of his own alienation as a learner and person. Schools are now a powerful agent in creating alienation in our society. Teachers feel alienated from themselves; and instead of existing as real persons to their students, they hide behind the facade of professional roles. We become alienated from our students, coworkers, and even from the subject matter we teach. If we are to change this object–object relationship with students, we first need to become real persons ourselves. We need to be more than professional people with degrees and credentials, with a mission to impart knowledge and skills to youth. What each must become is a being who can experience joy, sadness, despair, ecstasy, hope, love, tenderness, anger, loneliness, compassion, and the whole range of human experience. The choice is yours to make—whether you will be a thing or a person. While you can rationalize that your conditioning has contributed to your robot existence, when you become aware of this condition, choice does exist. There are no simple solutions to becoming human and overcoming the dehumanizing elements in your past. This is what each of us must struggle with. Moustakas contends that no matter how rigid, how mechanical, and how dehumanized a teacher has become, he still has the capacity to change.

He still can decide to alter his way of meeting others in the school setting, and can discover a more meaningful and genuine basis for involvement. He still can become the one he really is, and can actualize his potentialities as a whole, unified person. Regardless of past associations or fixations, the teacher can begin to view life freshly, can once more be in touch with the imaginative and creative resources of his own real self, can participate in the lives of other people as an authentic human being, open and aware of real meanings and values (86, p. 64).

The choice is ours to make. While the choice may involve anxiety and struggle, and the risks might be many, the unique personal identity could make this struggle worth the effort. What is a more rewarding project than becoming a fully functioning, alive, feeling, and total person?

FEELINGS ARE NOT IMPORTANT IN EDUCATION

One of the most damaging effects of traditional education is the preoccupation with the intellectual side of man to the exclusion of his emotional life. A. S. Neill, the founder of Summerhill, commented that what's wrong with most education is that it takes place from the neck up (34, 35). Neill feels that if we allow children to develop naturally, if we allow them the freedom to experience and own and express their feelings, the intellect will take care of itself. Hal Lyon, in his book *Learning to Feel—Feeling to Learn* (28), has descriptively painted a picture of the intellectual "half man." Our schools have contributed to the fractionalization of our minds and hearts. Years of conditioning have taught us that feelings have no legitimate place in the classroom. In fact, we are taught that feelings get in the way of learning, that emotions cloud clear thinking, that feelings ought to be denied, repressed, controlled, and carefully held in check. We are shown the value of being objective, and subjectivity is presented as something from which we ought to free ourselves so that we can become rational and objective in our pursuit of truth. As students we indirectly have received messages to divorce ourselves from our feelings. Consider some of the following statements, which we have all probably heard time and again:

- "Jim, what are you crying for? Big boys and men simply don't cry. Only babies cry!"
- "Now children, you shouldn't hate. We never hate people. God won't like us if we hate."
- "Don't be angry. If you get angry, I won't like you any more. It displeases me when you lose control. Keep your temper calm."
- "There now, Sonny, don't feel depressed. Count your blessings and be thankful for all you have instead of being sad."

- "I don't care how you feel about this poem; the most important thing is to understand what the poet had in mind as he wrote this piece."
- "Children, shame on you for fighting. Only animals, barbarians, and other uncivilized things resort to fighting to settle their differences."
- "Sally, you shouldn't feel jealous that your steady boyfriend is dating another girl. See everything in perspective."
- "I really don't care if you are upset or not because you didn't win the election for student body president. You have a job in this class, and you need to put your feelings aside and get to work."
- "People won't like you if you express negative feelings toward them. Always find something positive to say, or say nothing."
- "Sorry, students, but we don't have time to talk about sexual feelings in this Health Education class. Our course outline calls for learning the names and functions of the reproductive parts, nothing else!"
- "You need to learn to control your feelings. The trouble with people today is they can't control their emotions, and when emotions get out of hand, then there is chaos."
- "Don't worry about passing the College Board Exam. Worry never helps anybody. I'm sure everything will turn out O.K."

In my work as a college supervisor of student teachers, I've observed classrooms where young people were full of questions, enthusiasm, and feeling. And I've seen teachers nip any of this feeling in the bud. Once I visited a U.S. history class in which the teacher was pacing back and forth lecturing *at* his students in the same manner as his professors had lectured him. He was listing the Bill of Rights, and the students were to copy down his list faithfully. Several times a group of students genuinely wanted to discuss the clause pertaining to the freedom of speech. The student-teacher looked away, sternly stated that all he was interested in was that they memorized the list, not discuss their feelings about these statements. He had dozens of opportunities to convert his sterile lecture into an exciting and productive discussion of the meaning of the Bill of Rights. Instead, the students got the message that their feelings about the facts were unimportant.

In another instance, I was talking with a teacher who told me that her first grade class was watching the television broadcast of Robert Kennedy's funeral after his assassination. She admitted that she was astounded by the depth of her children's questions about death, and for a long time they showed an interest in learning more about death. She also admitted that she felt very guilty because she wasn't covering the math assignment that was on her schedule. One wonders whether her schedule was really that crucial, or whether her own fear of confronting her own feelings about death prevented her from exploring in depth with her children their interests at that time.

Our education has in many ways taught us to be distrusting of our feelings. We value our intellect; and in this process we have separated our intellect from our emotional life. We have become numb to what we feel. When someone asks us how we *feel,* we usually tell them what we *think.* The sad reality is that we lose the ability to be aware that we are out of touch with our own feelings.

Consider this background with which you have been reared both in school and at home. If you have become detached from your own feelings, if you have learned to fear feelings, distrust them, repress or deny or distort them, and if you keep feelings tightly bottled up inside of you, how can you expect to accept realistically or deal with the depth and intensity of the feelings of the children or adolescents you teach? If you deny your own feelings, can you really *allow* your students to express their feelings openly? What value is an education that teaches us to divorce ourselves from our experience? In a way, were we not in a more advantageous position *before* we entered school? Don't most children, before they become "socialized," have the precious capacity to experience and own their feelings? What happens to us that we begin to think that feelings are bad? How difficult it is for most of us to unlearn old ways and to relearn something we once knew as children! Before concluding this section, I urge you to consider these questions seriously as they affect you in your personal life as a teacher:

- Can you experience anxiety and deal with it constructively, or do you find yourself denying anxiety by burying yourself in busy work?
- Can you accept your own anger? Are you able to be aware when you are angry? Can you express it, or do you find ways to seal off angry feelings?
- Have you faced your own eventual nonbeing? Do you deny your anxiety related to death and dying?
- Are you able to experience a range and depth of feelings, or do you retreat from situations involving emotional intensity?
- Are you able to experience depression, sadness, hopelessness, meaninglessness, and despair at times? Are you able to deal with these feelings creatively?
- Do you ever experience joy, ecstasy, and delight? Are you able to spontaneously *be* your feelings?

- Have you ever really *felt* and experienced failure? Do you have to succeed at all times? When you fail, what is the experience like, and how do you deal with these feelings?
- Can you experience solitude and still enjoy your own company? Can you feel alive when you are alone—without people, television, books, activities, and other ways of escaping from yourself?
- To what degree are you able to tolerate ambiguity and the lack of clear structure in your daily living? Can you tolerate uncertainty, confusion, and change?
- Have you ever experienced love *from* another person? Have you genuinely loved and really cared about another person?
- Are you able to *feel* a sense of self-worth, dignity, and respect for yourself?
- To what degree are you able to experience your own sexuality? Can you *be* your sexual feelings, and can you *own* these feelings? Do you deny, distort, and repress sexual feelings?
- Do you feel comfortable with the kind of man or woman you are? Do you *feel* masculine or feminine?
- Are you able at times to be a child and an adolescent? Have you become so "adult" that you have lost touch with the child and adolescent that still reside in you?

While this list of questions for self-examination could be extended, the main point I am attempting to make is this: How can we expect to understand or accept our students as feeling persons if we cannot come to terms with our own emotions? If my thesis is true, and teachers have lost contact with directly experiencing their feelings, then doesn't it make sense that as teachers we will experience real difficulty in tuning into the *feelings* of our students? How can we help our students deal with their feelings of failure, defeat, and frustration if we escape from these feelings ourselves? If we feel ill at ease with our own sexual feelings, is it really possible to deal honestly with the sexual concerns of students? If we are unable to tolerate ambiguity or disorganization in our own lives, how are we able to deal with the anxiety of students when they face ambiguity? If we bury all of our negative feelings, pretend they do not exist, then how can we react to children when they explode with anger, rage, or hostility?

TEACHERS—KEEP YOUR DISTANCE FROM STUDENTS

As students we learn our place and our role in relationship to our teachers. There are numerous devices that put distance between teachers and students. When we finally sit on the other side of the desk, we adopt the same kind of professional role that creates a social distance between us and the learner. Unfortunately, even in teacher training departments, teacher interns are admonished:

- Don't reveal your personal life to your students. Keep your personal life separate and away from school.
- Don't smile before Christmas! Show the kids that you're tough and mean business.
- Do not touch your students either in anger or in tenderness. Remember the possibility of lawsuits.
- Don't get too personal with students. They want a teacher, not a friend.
- Stick to the subject you are paid to teach.
- Be objective, impartial, fair, and consistent.
- You shouldn't have feelings of favoritism; if you do, surely never show them.
- Be professional. Keep a psychological reserve about you and maintain proper social distance.
- Don't become angry in the classroom. If you should get angry, don't show it openly.
- Never reveal your basic values regarding your personal beliefs on religion, politics, morality, or human affairs.
- It's best to be safe and not discuss sex, religion, or politics in class.
- Politely let the students know that these touchy issues are not appropriate topics for classroom discussion.
- Learn to hide your feelings if they are negative. Children need to be protected from a teacher's feelings.

These are merely a few of the myths that teachers acquire during their training years. Unfortunately, far too many teachers cling to these myths as though they were reality, surely blocking the way to person-to-person relationships.

Perhaps the reason we cling to these myths is because we don't want to change. Some people become teachers because they want to feel superior to students. If they shrink this social distance, and if they relate to students in an equal manner as persons, then they can no longer be superior. I am suggesting that we focus upon the way we do relate to our students, and that we consider the rewards of encountering students "straight across" as equals—as people with dignity, respect, and worth. If we can *genuinely* interact with students as equal persons, the response we receive from them is rewarding. Children and adolescents do not appreciate an adult who "tries too hard" to be "one of them"; and they resent and ridicule adults who are phony in attempting to be popular and universally liked. But they do have admiration, respect, trust, and even love for adults who are secure enough in their own personal development to put aside stereotyped roles and become authentic persons. Students cry out for teachers who are human and humane; they seek out adults who will listen to them and respect their views; they are asking for adults who will respect them and care about them as individuals; they do not want their teacher to be a God, a computer, or some distant professional who will "help" them. Most of the students I encounter simply want a teacher who will not be afraid of them and not be afraid to *be* a person instead of a role. Is this asking too much? Can we perform the functions expected of us as teachers and still operate on a human level with young people?

Before moving to another topic, I should like to recommend Herbert Kohl's captivating book *36 Children* (46) to every teacher. I'm impressed with the person of Herb Kohl as revealed through his writings. Here is a man that did make himself known to his students. He disclosed himself and shared his goals, dreams, struggles, joys, and anxieties with the children in his classroom. His colleagues called his exposure "unprofessional." Could it be that they were seriously threatened by Kohl's shedding of an authority role? How could they keep this social distance if teachers begin to get too close to students? Kohl admits that he did make mistakes. He had an open-door policy at his house; before long, he was swamped with his children visiting him. His private life became almost nil. Kohl does suggest that we need to become involved, but we also need to retain our privacy. "I had to set limits on what I could do as an individual and have always had to balance what part of my life I could offer the children, and what part had to remain private" (p. 108).

SCHOOL TEACHES US TO BE DISHONEST

Though many parents and teachers still argue this point, I believe that because school is a dishonest place, it teaches us to be dishonest. In Holt's *How Children Fail* (6, pp. 170–73), he remarks that school is a dishonest place because

We tell students what to think and feel;
We tell them not what we think, but what we feel they ought to think;
We are not honest with ourselves with students;
We present ourselves to children as if we are gods;
We are dishonest with our feelings;
Since we are not honest with children, we won't let them be honest with us!

We give lip service to ideals of honesty, integrity, trust, and democracy, but by our actions we really demonstrate a basic dishonesty. How many teachers are willing to be honest with their students on issues related to their values? How many of us are willing to risk revealing our real thoughts and feelings on sensitive issues? As a rationalization we blame our narrow-minded administrators or "uptight" parents. Isn't this often a real cover for the reality that we simply do not want to take personal responsibility?

In *36 Children* (46) Kohl emphasizes how essential it is to be honest with children. "No hypocrite can win the respect of children, and without respect, one cannot teach" (p. 19). Kohl also suggests that we need to be able to make mistakes, that we can be human and not superhuman, and that students respect us for attempting to work toward greater honesty. He says: "It is the teacher's struggle to be moral that excites his pupils. It is his honesty, not rightness, that moves children" (p. 26).

If you agree with my opinion that schools teach us to be dishonest, the next question is: "O.K., so I agree, but what can I do about it?" I think we can begin by learning to accept the reality that none of us are fully congruent, authentic, and real persons. In all of us there is some phoniness. What we can do is learn to detect when we are being unreal, not congruent, and dishonest. What I see as the real task is to become honest with ourselves. We desperately attempt to fool and convince ourselves of our realness. But we can work toward remaining open, toward allowing ourselves to be challenged; and we can begin to admit to others when we sense that we are being dishonest. The implications for teachers in terms of building trusting, honest, and open relationships are vast. Sometimes as teachers we must do things in our classrooms that we do not fully support. Examples might be administering statewide standardized tests, submitting course grades, requiring a final examination, and covering certain required topics. We can at least be honest with our students and let them in on our feelings. This may not seem vastly important, but it does open the door to a more authentic way of relating with students.

STUDENTS ARE NOT TO BE TRUSTED

I have come to believe firmly that educators (as a group) have the philosophy that man is basically evil. Man is viewed as inherently weak, with inclinations toward laziness, aggression, intolerance, and selfishness. Left to his own devices man will become self-destructive and social disorder will prevail. This philosophy of man is related to the philosophy expressed in *Lord of the Flies,* that children are basically savages who need to be socialized, regulated, controlled, motivated, directed, rewarded, punished, and kindly manipulated so that their evil nature does not become predominant.

Educators feel that young learners need external motivation in order to sustain learning activity. Our experience in school has taught us that left alone we will not learn; we need clear structuring and direction; we cannot handle freedom to learn; being told what to do, and when to do it, is more comforting than finding our own way. Leonard describes most schools as unfit places for learning, because they resemble jails more than learning centers (14). He adds that most classrooms are set up to prevent thinking, learning, and creativity. Schools, according to Leonard, emphasize classroom control and conformity; students learn to sit still, form orderly rows, take instructions, and feel guilty about their natural impulses.

Other provocative authors have written books which deal with the theme of students being treated more like prisoners than learners. Holt, in *The Underachieving School* (8), says that teaching is secondary to the babysitting function. He charges schools with mouthing democratic values, while in reality students learn "practical slavery"! Holt observes that "schools are bad places for kids," and that children are smarter, more curious, more eager, and less afraid *before* starting school than after they enter school. Edgar Friedenberg's *Coming of Age in America* (3) is a criticism of public secondary education. He, too, feels that the rights of students have been denied, that students are treated as lowly citizens, and that high schools resemble jails. The students, like prisoners, are "marking time" while waiting for their sentences to end.

A. S. Neill, in *Summerhill* (35), vividly describes what children are like who come to his school from repressive, authoritarian backgrounds. Neill has established a true free school where a philosophy based upon trust of children is practiced. Neill feels that children are basically good, that they need freedom to grow, that given true freedom they can become self-regulated individuals, and that children *do* have the desire to learn about life. Carl Rogers has written an entire book devoted to encouraging teachers to provide a climate of freedom for the learner. In his *Freedom to Learn* (31), Rogers says that if even one teacher in one hundred would have student-centered classrooms where students are allowed genuine freedom to pursue personally relevant issues, education in this country could be revolutionized. He forcefully makes the case that even when you might expect the greatest degree of freedom to be granted (at the graduate school), the assumption is still made that learners do not have the capacity to learn without outside direction and without external evaluation.

Even with my graduate classes in educational psychology, I hear statements from my students such as: "But aren't children too young and immature to set their own goals?" "Won't chaos be the result if we let students do as they please?" "And what will happen to our students if we *do* grant them freedom? How will they adjust when they go out into society?" "But can we expect students to want to learn what they *need* to learn?" "Wouldn't they take the easy way out?" "At what age are they ready for freedom? Can they handle freedom? Will they run wild and abuse any freedom I give them?" "Well, I know for me that if I were not *forced* to study I would have simply done nothing!"

Perhaps this last statement gives a real indication of why many teachers basically do not trust students. When they reflect on their own school experience they see how much was forced upon them. Since they had little investment in their own education, they took advantage of opportunities to dodge working. So they assume that the students they teach are out to get by with minimum investment in their classes. By God, they'll show them who is smarter! They won't let them get away with goofing off in their rooms! And so the stupid game of teacher tries to outsmart student and student tries to outfox teacher goes on. A way to break the game is to develop a trusting attitude toward students and let them select at least some of their own learning goals. If a student has personal involvement in an activity, we are not needed as motivators.

Let me clarify my concept of freedom. What I am advocating is a degree of genuine freedom for the learner where he becomes a partner in his learning journey. The learner has some say in topics he wants to learn and some voice in the way he learns and in the evaluation of his learning. So often the graduate students I work with equate freedom with license. I am advocating freedom *with responsibility*. We ought to grant as much freedom as the learner *and* the teacher can realistically handle. If we have been reared with the attitude that we cannot be trusted with our own learning, we are generally authoritarian in the way we conduct our classes. We teach the way we were taught, unfortunately.

What implications can be drawn from all of this? First of all, teachers need to recognize to what degree they have been trusted as individuals and as students, and to what degree they are now trusted as professional people. It is imperative that they become conscious of their philosophy of man and of education also. If we cling to the notion of man's inherent evil, then I see little hope for any substantial reform. However, if we can genuinely believe in the capacity of the individual to work toward ends which are self-enhancing, then we can design a different type of learning environment. Even the most rigid teacher can make a beginning by providing a *small* degree of authentic freedom. I suggest experimentation by granting a measure of freedom and then observing the effects. We need to be patient—both with ourselves and our students. It will take time. Struggle, conflict, anxiety, and insecurity are essential side results of releasing *real* freedom. From my experience with high school and college students, I strongly believe that they are aware of limitations of their freedom. They realize that a teacher has certain restraints placed upon him; and they can understand that there may be some policies that neither the students nor teacher can circumvent. It is essential that we discuss our feelings about working toward a freer and more open classroom.

We can all begin to move away from a teacher-centered classroom where the dictum is "the teacher knows best," to a student-centered classroom where students are viewed with the expectation that they *can* make wise choices, and they can choose among alternatives, and they can take responsibility for their own choices. I like Kohl's hints in his book *The Open Classroom* (45). One of his suggestions is to provide ten minutes a day of true free time. Watch what happens and gradually increase this free time. As Kohl suggests, though, unless we are deeply dissatisfied with conventional education, there is little hope for changing a teacher-dominated classroom into an open classroom.

In *Freedom to Learn* (31) Rogers describes an experiment with Miss Barbara Shiels, a fourth grade teacher with thirteen years of experience as she faced a frustrating class. There was no evidence of any real learning; enthusiasm and morale were low; there were discipline problems. Miss Shiels dared to venture forth and grant these young learners more freedom. She allowed them to select topics and subjects that interested them. With each student she worked out contracts. Students were involved in the assessment of their own work. While her experiment caused uncertainty and anxiety (for both the students and the teacher), it was a success. The children learned, they were enthusiastic, and they were able to use the freedom allowed constructively. One central point: students often meet the expectancies of their teachers. Barbara Shiels expected her children to handle their freedom successfully. She had faith in her children as learners, and faith in her own ability as a facilitator of learning. Perhaps this is the crucial element. If we see students as basically untrustworthy, could it be that they are living up to our expectations of them? And if we can *trust* ourselves enough so that we can begin to have faith in our students, then isn't there a good possibility that they might amaze us with their ability? Chances are they will exceed our wildest fantasies of what they might become!

SUMMARY AND FOCUS

Essentially I encourage you to reflect upon your own school years with the aim of becoming more aware of the messages communicated to you as a learner. Early in the education game we learn that pleasing the teacher is what really counts. Instead of looking inward and discovering our own unique identities, we are conditioned to seek external direction for our valuing and behaving. By never questioning the authority figures, we become "good" students and we are on our way to becoming "successful" students. We become conformists, and in doing so, lose touch with our separate individuality.

Soon we learn that competition is a part of the American way of life. Before we enter school we are eager, curious, and flexible learners. But as we become "schooled," our education teaches us to work for extrinsic rewards. The aim of the game is to beat the next guy's performance.

In learning to be successful students we quickly become aware that there are right answers to every problem. We become passive, and in this passivity we do what is expected of us. More and more, we fear freedom and cling to secure paths outlined by the teacher. Instead of learning how to learn, and learning a process for further inquiry, most of our energies are directed toward arriving at correct answers. We lose faith in ourselves and in our ability to think critically.

School is something that is separate from our outside life. Much of our learning is only apparent learning, bits of unorganized information which has little relevance for life. Our time in school is spent in learning about everything except about ourselves. Questions on the meaning of our existence are considered minor. There is little personal involvement or commitment to education since the self of the learner is denied. We are treated more like objects than persons—objects to be manipulated by those who have our "best interests at heart." This contributes to feelings of alienation and depersonalization.

Schools concentrate mainly upon our intellectual nourishment; in so doing, feelings are left out of our education. We learn that our feelings are relatively unimportant, with the result that we become half persons. We also learn to keep our distance from our teachers. As a result of this distance, teachers rarely become real persons to us; instead they are perceived as nonpersons.

You are taught dishonesty in schools. And with this teaching you are encouraged to go along with the game. In many ways, you are told that you are not really to be trusted as learners. Freedom is something that you cannot handle, so you are told and directed. This entire process produces a learner who is an intellectual and emotional cripple. But there is hope. If you can understand the effects of your education, then perhaps you can change. The choice is yours. You *can* become carbon copies of the teachers you had, or you can transcend this conditioning and provide a vastly different kind of education for the students you teach.

3

Teachers Can Make a Difference

WHY PEOPLE BECOME TEACHERS

Sometime during the professional teacher preparation program, each candidate is asked the question "Why do you want to become a teacher?" It is only a rare person who can come up with an honest answer to this inquiry. Why not try a simple test before reading ahead. Sit alone for about ten minutes and reflect upon some of your basic reasons for wanting to become a teacher. Then jot down all the various motives that might account for why you selected teaching as a career. Before you finish this exercise, look over your list and attempt to classify how many motives are based upon "helping others" and how many reasons relate to your own personal need satisfaction. I'll be willing to wager that most of your reasons sound altruistic, and that it is far easier to itemize factors that relate to serving others than to list those that relate to serving yourself.

A thesis I'd like to explore is that many people become teachers mainly to satisfy their own psychological needs, often for selfish reasons, though they somehow have a need to convince themselves of their unselfish love for mankind. Many who enter teaching or other helping professions have a real need to convert others, help humanity, and in some way change the world. In working closely with teacher preparation students, I've learned how difficult it is for most people to accept the *personal* motivations apart from serving others. Let me discuss in more detail some of the psychological dynamics that operate in the lives of teachers.

THE NEED TO BE NEEDED

Many teachers thrive on the need to have their students depend upon them. It's a rewarding feeling to know that others really need us. And surely it is even more rewarding if our students admire, love, and respect us. With this model, the teacher is the one who gives generously and our pupils take out of our abundance. But I suspect that in this kind of "unselfish giving" we are really receiving all kinds of need gratification. In fact, we actually depend upon our pupils to be dependent. How else could we give? It doesn't take much insight to become aware of how the giver is the superior person. This can elevate our feelings of self-worth and importance. Even if the rest of the world doesn't love us or recognize our true value, we can bask with the consoling thought that our students love and need us. What I am saying may seem rather negative, but my point is that blocking this from awareness can be harmful. It is analogous to the giving mother who in a self-sacrificing style devotes her total energy to rearing her children. She lives for them and through them as well. What a burden to place upon children! This "love" breeds guilt feelings when the children finally emerge toward autonomy. And the other problem is what becomes of the mother when her reason for being (taking care of the children) no longer is in force. Does the mother's meaning in life cease when her children leave? Similarly, teachers can easily be too wrapped up in serving the needs of pupils (and thus themselves feeling important). This needing to be needed results in retardation of the autonomy of the learner.

THE NEED FOR PERSONAL COMPETENCE

Another factor that drives people to a helping profession is the need for a feeling of personal competence. Routinely I ask my students who expect to become teachers to review their own past experiences as a learner—from the earliest contact with school to the present—and to fantasize what it felt like to be a learner at each grade level. No longer am I surprised at the number of people reporting negative experiences. Sometimes this is a painful process. In getting in touch with our own feelings of loneliness, anxiety, failure as learners, we might say, "When I become a teacher, I am *not* going to make the same mistakes that I experienced with my teachers."

When you earn your teaching credentials, and you are on the other side of the desk, some strange feelings occur. Your role as teacher guarantees you some measure of competence. Now you have power that you might never have known before. I suggest that there are more than a few who become teachers because of this power. They become the authority figure against whom they reacted for so many years.

THE NEED FOR POWER

Teachers are potentially powerful people. They have the power to open unknown avenues and invite learners to explore these paths. Also they have power to destroy what creative spark might exist in a child. They *do* possess power either to facilitate the actualization of a child's potential or to stifle this innate curiosity. While teachers have this potential power, my experience is that teachers (as a group) act and feel as though they were powerless. They continually look outside of themselves for justification of these feelings of impotence. If only their principal were not so authoritarian. If only they didn't have to worry about tenure, about promotions, about disconcerted parents, about rigid policies, about grumbling students! If only . . . then, they would be magnificent teachers! Then they could really be inventive, daring, and exciting! My question is why we can't *use* our own power to cope with and overcome these obstacles. Why do we allow our destiny to be shaped by others? Why do we seem to tolerate our impotence?

Frequently people who *feel* powerless, inadequate, inferior, and insecure emotionally and socially are actually attracted to the profession of teaching. In their role as teachers, they can feel like the top dog intellectually, and they gain a false sense of superiority by wielding their power over the underdog student. Where else can a person find unchallenged authority? Isn't it gratifying to be a giant among dwarfs? Is it not rewarding for the inadequate person to keep his subordinates under control, to discipline them, to treat them harshly? Where else has this person experienced such toughness, such strength, such superiority? The destructive element, of course, is that this sense of power grows out of weakness, and it is a defense against impotence. The teacher uses the feeling of power over subordinates to compensate for his feeling powerless in the face of his (real or imagined) superiors. And the only way such a teacher can maintain this sense of potency is by keeping his students in subordinate position. Since the growth of his students is a threat to this teacher's potency, the students *must* remain inferior as persons. Unfortunately, the school system now fosters innumerable power props that keep power-hungry teachers well fed.

THE NEED FOR SECURITY

People who are security-hungry often find the teaching profession most satisfying; for until recently, teachers were greatly in demand. The individual who is overly concerned about security rarely takes any risks. He dares not offend an administrator. He becomes whatever the powers that be expect of him. He is not a rocker of the boat; since waves make him nauseated, he sails only in calm waters. He avoids lively debate in his classroom on any sensitive controversial issue. He follows the book, rarely behaves spontaneously, consistently chooses the safe path, and doesn't irritate his superiors until he is protected with his hard-earned tenure. Chances are that even when the security-minded teacher has this tenure, he will continue to behave as before. One who sells his soul seldom recaptures it upon the awarding of tenure.

Now in many suburbs and cities young people are finding themselves with newly-issued teaching credentials, but without teaching contracts. I see this tightening of the marketplace as desirable, for as competition becomes keener, we can afford to be more discriminating in hiring effective teachers. I'm not suggesting reckless living where we ignore legitimate needs for security and stability. My point is that if we are so insecure that we rarely risk losing security, we become dull, lifeless, apathetic, and ineffectual in our work. We need to challenge our stability by not compromising on crucial issues. This implies that each of us decides for ourselves what areas we can compromise on and still retain our integrity, and the areas where we must remain solid.

If there are side benefits gained by being a teacher, fine. My concern is for the students who are unfortunate enough to have a teacher who is motivated *primarily* by the insurance of a steady income, a job with long vacations, and a job that does not make unusual demands upon the person.

THE SECONDARY BENEFITS OF TEACHING

It is said that a person who flunked law school can find refuge as a social studies teacher; the would-be biologist who wasn't accepted in a Ph.D. program might teach health education; the frustrated actor or actress who couldn't make it in professional life turns to coaching drama as a second choice; and the engineer or businessman who lost his job in the "real world" begrudgingly accepts teaching as his only out.

We all have heard the saying "Those who can, do; and those who can't, teach." Thinking about some teachers whom I have encountered, I shudder as I admit to at least the partial truth there. I'm idealistic enough to expect our profession to be staffed with people who want to be educators first. I've heard teacher candidates admit:

> "Well, my kids are grown-up now, my husband would like me to work, so I decided to come back to college and finish up my degree and get my credential as soon as possible so that we can supplement our income."
> "I'm studying to become a teacher so that in case my husband dies, I can always fall back on teaching."

"I'm not really enthused about the prospect of standing in front of a class of brats all day, but what else can a woman major in nowadays in college?"

"Well, frankly, thinking of myself as a future teacher really doesn't turn me on, but I really groove on getting out of work by 2:30, the Christmas and Easter vacations, and the three months off in summer-time."

"You know, school is really a drag and I've never really enjoyed going to school or reading, or even learning—but I figure that I can always find a steady job somewhere as a teacher."

"I really don't know why I am in college and why I'm working on my credential. I suppose it is because my folks always expected me to become a teacher."

Again, I'm not suggesting that we discount some real advantages afforded by the teaching profession. My fear is that if our main motivation in selecting this career is based upon these secondary gains, we will probably succeed in turning off far more learners than we turn on.

I see our profession as demanding, often times draining and exhausting, and one that simply requires a good bit of dedication. Commitment is essential. Good teaching is difficult. The kind of effort needed to reach learners simply cannot be generated by individuals who are marginally committed to their profession. What I am requesting is that we seek individuals who are genuinely interested in learning themselves and who have a primary concern in the facilitation of the learning of others.

HEALTHY MOTIVATIONS FOR BECOMING A TEACHER

We have looked at some common dynamics involved in selecting teaching as a vocation. I have indicated that many people seek teaching as a way of being needed. By giving constantly to others, we achieve a sense of superiority and a sense that we are useful and helpful. Through teaching we might discover a sense of power that we never believed possible. Let me stress that all of these needs—for power, personal competence, for being needed, for security, and for being appreciated—are not neurotic reasons for becoming a teacher. My point is that when these needs are based upon basic feelings of inadequacy, then the teacher is in trouble. When teaching becomes the exclusive avenue by which he acquires a sense of power, and when he feels powerless when he is not playing a teacher role, then there is difficulty. The danger is when a teacher's identity as a person is almost totally dependent upon his being "teacher." Apart from this narrow role, he dries up and become a non-person. Let us now examine a more positive dimension of selecting teaching as a career.

THE TEACHER WHO MAKES A DIFFERENCE IN THE LIVES OF STUDENTS

To me, a healthy reason for remaining in the teaching profession is a teacher's awareness that he is making a significant difference in the lives of his students. Surely, no teacher will reach and touch every one of his students, but the realization that some of our students are more enriched as persons because of their relationships with us is probably one of the most attractive aspects of our profession.

At this point, I suggest that you reflect upon the few (or many if you are fortunate) teachers you have encountered who have significantly changed your life—the ones that helped you to reach far more of your potential—and those who were influential in your becoming a more complete person. Recall what they were like as persons. What did they mean to you? Why were they able to reach you—and how did they do so? What effect do they have on your life now? How are you the person you are as a partial result of their influence in your life? What kinds of changes in your life did they foster?

I want to raise some questions related to a model for the kind of teacher who makes a significant difference in the lives of the students he encounters. Perhaps I should begin with a few words on what this model is not. I wish to emphasize that this is not a model of perfection, and this is not a stagnant or completed product. In fact, the teacher who is convinced that he *is* self-actualized, fully mature, nearly completely contented, with merely a few minor flaws, is the one who worries me the most. This is a smug, self-satisfied, complacent person who has probably given up struggling toward fuller growth. Besides, how can students possibly identify with a "perfect" person? I'm convinced that it's not a teacher's degree of perfection that earns the student's respect; rather it is experiencing a teacher who is actively and honestly working toward the process of becoming a more enriched and alive human that really counts. It is a teacher who is truly struggling to become more aware, more honest with himself and others, who influences students in a therapeutic way.

Let me propose the following questions with the suggestion that you reflect and honestly attempt to answer them for yourself. A word of caution: try to avoid answering as you think you should, or even as you would like to be able to answer them. Instead, try to give an answer that reflects where you are *now*.

- Am I really doing anything to insure my personal growth or do I secretly believe that I am a fairly self-actualized person?
- Do I demand very much for myself from life? Am I satisfied with accepting what I now have instead of working toward becoming more as a person?
- To what degree am I expanding my own awareness of my own needs? Am I doing anything to enlarge my knowledge of myself and my personal world?
- Am I able to experience a range of feelings? Am I in touch with what I feel? Can I express my feelings freely if I so choose?
- Do I accept the "child" in me and the "adolescent" in me, or have I become adult to the point where I must stifle these parts of me?
- To what degree do I like myself? Do I have a sense of self-worth, dignity, and love of self? How can I genuinely appreciate another person if I do not appreciate myself?
- Do I feel a sense of zest and enthusiasm for my work? Am I able to become excited about my work, or is it merely a boring routine?
- Can I have fun—and can I enjoy present moments? Can I really allow myself to enjoy myself with my friends, spouse, children, students?
- Am I able to accept myself as I am, that is, recognize who I am and what I am, or do I find ways of denying parts of my being?
- What am I actually doing about changing myself in a direction that I want to move toward? Do I simply say I wish I were different, but do little about making any changes?
- Is most of my life based upon meeting others' expectations and standards of me, or am I truly attempting to define and live by my own expectations?
- How do I feel about my own sexuality? Am I satisfied with the kind of man or woman I am? Do I deny, hide, or distort my sexuality?
- Do I care enough about myself to be selfish? Can I recognize my own needs, and meet them; or am I the self-sacrificing type who is selfless in thinking only of others?
- Whom do I love? How do I show and evidence this love? How loved do I feel?
- Do I spend any time meditating upon questions such as who am I? What do I want from life? What do I want to give life? What do I value most?
- Do I arrange my life in such a way that I escape from being alone? Or do I value alone time and use it as a source of renewing my life and getting in touch with my values?
- Am I a congruent person; that is, am I able to show the self that I really am to others? Is there a wide gap between what I am privately like and what I publicly present?
- To what degree am I able to fully experience the present? Am I

bound by the past, by what I should have done? Ought to have done? Am I so future-oriented that I allow the intensity of the *now* slip by?

- Have I developed or am I developing a system of values that give my life direction, meaning, and purpose? Is this value system an open one that allows for growth, or is my value system relatively fixed?
- Do I really care about others, or do I merely pretend to care? How do I give evidence of the quality of my caring?
- Am I aware of my hang-ups and how these personal problems interfere with my relationships with my students?
- Can I allow my students the freedom to become what they choose to become or do I have a need to mold them into a form which I consider to be good for them?
- To what degree am I open to new experiences? What specific ways do I avail myself of new experience, and what ways do I close myself to the unknown?
- Can I live with ambiguity? Can I tolerate living without sureness? What in my life testifies to the degree that I can tolerate lack of clarity?

TEACHERS AS THERAPEUTIC PERSONS

We have examined some healthy and some not so healthy reasons for being a teacher. The central motive for remaining in teaching that I see as healthy is that of actually becoming a therapeutic person who influences students in a growth-oriented way toward becoming more complete persons. To feel and know that we can be human instruments in effecting a significant difference in a student's life can be one of the most rewarding aspects of teaching. Let me describe my thoughts regarding what a therapeutic teacher is like. Surely my list is incomplete, but here I am attempting to generate thought. I recommend you add your own thoughts to this partial list. When I think of a teacher who is a therapeutic person, and who facilitates the personal growth of students, here is what comes to my mind as a list of personal qualities and characteristics:

- A person who has found his own way. He does not imitate another's style, and he teaches in a way that is compatible with his own personality.
- A person who appreciates and respects himself. This person can give out of his strength, and not "give" to receive a false feeling of strength. He is able to be powerful, and at the same time not diminish others in order to feel adequate.

- One who is open to change, generally in touch with self, and willing to risk for more. Rather than settling for less, this person will extend himself to become more.
- An inner-directed person who has engaged in challenging his value system; one who lives from internal standards rather than what others expect.
- One who has an identity. He knows who he is, what he is capable of becoming, what he wants out of life, and what's essential. He questions life. This is not a fixed position; rather the person is at least engaged in confronting himself with these questions.
- A person who acts in a way in which he believes, even though he might not be encouraged or rewarded for his beliefs and actions.
- One who genuinely wants to relate to students as persons; one who shares at least parts of his humanness with them.
- A person who has empathy. He can crawl inside the shoes of students and experience the feelings as they do. He has not forgotten his own struggles, so he can relate personally to his students.
- One who has a life outside of teaching. He has a circle of people who care about him and about whom he cares. He has interests separate from that of teaching.
- The person who is sincere and honest. He does not pretend to be that which he is not.
- A person who is alive! He feels intensely and generally enjoys life. He can feel a range of emotions from elation to depression.

A SEASONED TEACHER GETS EXCITED BY 36 CHILDREN

As an example of a teacher who is open to change and does seem to be making a difference with her school children, I'd like to share a paper I received from a "seasoned" teacher—a woman with considerable teaching experience who was close to retirement, yet still searching for more dynamic ways of reaching her children. In one of my workshop courses for teachers, she read Kohl's book *36 Children* (46), and was inspired to integrate some of his methods in her own classroom. This is proof that a teacher who is willing to experiment and trust both herself and the children can affect positive changes in learning. Read on to sense the enthusiasm and courage to risk something new:

> It would be impossible to have found a book that could have been more helpful or meaningful to me at this time than the book *36 Children*. This past year I was given a group of twenty-two very low achievers to form a remedial reading class for the lowest seventh grade readers. Such classes always challenge me, but this group appeared literally impossible. All had accepted failure as their level of

operation—all had given up being able to read above a third grade level, and in all, it looked hopeless. I understood perfectly what Mr. Kohl was saying about his frustrations at facing his group in Harlem.

Accepting my frustration as real and finding that none of the old "tried-and-true" methods could work, I approached my principal about releasing me to experiment. He was only too eager to have me launch out, and this I did. The children chose their own books and wrote papers and letters or whatever inspired them as they read. The room was busily noisy at times and very still at other times—but everyone was reading or writing or communicating. What excitement! These kids loved their reading class! I moved among them asking them questions, suggesting when necessary and just communicating with the kids if this was what they needed.

The district's finest substitute nearly went mad the first few days she had the group—but learning *was* going on!

Oh, that I'd had Mr. Kohl's book to give me new ideas and suggestions on his many ingenious methods of teaching! I felt lost at times, because other teachers openly doubted what I was doing with these children. Never have I read a book on education where I so fully identified with the author! I felt his frustration and helplessness. I felt with him the tug of tradition and the old right way to run a classroom. As I read about Maurice, Pamela, Robert, and Alvin, I could see my children in action. I grew so excited about what was happening to Mr. Kohl's children, I had to share it with everyone in my household. It was a fabulous experience!

As I went through the book, I wrote out the procedures I feel will be valuable to me this coming year. I found suggestions that I catalogued under the following headings: (a) Concepts of Early Man, (b) Sociological Understanding, (c) Development of Self-Worth and Esteem, (d) Study of Architecture and Design, (e) Vocabulary Development, (f) Journalism, (g) Study of Mythology, and (h) Teaching International Relationships. There are many more I want to go back and glean from the book.

From my brief adventure into this new field of teaching through experience and self-exploration and self-fulfillment, I have consented to teach three classes of a course my principal and I are going to call "Communications." This can be reading, writing, journalism, drama, research, or what have you, in areas the child chooses.

So intrigued was my principal with my adventure in teaching remedial reading with individual interest determining the curriculum for each child, and giving the child the freedom to explore, that he has asked me to use the same methods in teaching this new course called "Communications."

In testing these remedial readers, the lowest group in school, we found more gains and greater gains than we had realized in any of the other reading classes. One boy moved from 3.2 grade level to 7.8 grade level during the year. Others made lesser gains. We gave no grades, but we all read and grew in self-worth and self-acceptance, as well as in reading skills.

Herbert Kohl's book was so honest, so transparent, and so warm with feeling. He dared to be different to meet the needs of his children. His own personal growth, as well as that of the children's, were humbly displayed as he wrote. It will prove a guidebook for me next year. I hope that I may be as honest with my frustrations and weaknesses as he was, so that I might grow through the adventures that await me.

STUDENT VIEWS ON TEACHERS WHO MAKE A DIFFERENCE

In concluding this chapter, we will look at the kinds of characteristics that high school students say they look for in their teachers. if we want to know the kind of teacher the students want, then we ought to ask them. This is what I have done. High school students in four different high schools were asked to repond anonymously to the following three questions:

1. What are some characteristics you look for in a teacher? What is your idea of a truly outstanding teacher? What is he or she like as a person?
2. What do you most want from your teacher?
3. What are some things that bother you the most about teachers in general?

Students can teach us a lot, if only we will listen. These student responses are presented exactly as they wrote them, without "correction" and without discussion. It is hoped that they will sensitize us to what students are really saying. These students are all sophomores, juniors, or seniors in public high schools.

QUESTION: *What are some characteristics you look for in a teacher? What is your idea of a truly outstanding teacher? What is he or she like as a person?*

STUDENT REPLIES

- I think being able to laugh with the students and identify with them is one thing that's important. They have to be honest to the students and give them a chance without having to think that the teacher will jump on them if they don't agree. An outstanding teacher must have these qualities and they can't be plastic people.

- Understanding, honest, sense of humor, sufficient knowledge of subject being taught, sufficient knowledge in general, some knowledge of life, (optional, but helps) dresses well, teacher that will help you not only with studies but personally *when you need it.*
- Trust, reliability, stick-to-itiveness, poise, firm but nice, ability to handle a class, a just person not one who picks favorites. One who can talk to the class about pertinent subjects and who can teach the kids so they *learn.* He or she isn't fake but the same way all the time.
- I look for a smile and a neat looking person. An outstanding teacher is one who talks on your level and understanding. The person is a warm person.
- A teacher that is open, and yet will take suggestions is a good start. Closed-minded people tend to have difficulty with large groups of people and usually don't make good teachers.
- Acting like a real person instead of a superior, and being able to answer your question in your language. To just answer your questions, and not make a big issue out of it if you don't understand. She or he should just be able to get through to the students. Now I'd like to you to tell me how many people get to know their teacher as a person?
- Someone easy, free and fun. Someone I can talk to and kid. Someone I can feel is really my age, someone I don't feel like I have to look up to. I don't like to feel that I should respect adults just because they're adults. I respect them when they earn it.
- She trusts, loves, understands, doen't act like she is the educator and your the idiot that must be taught, one that I go and talk to, she listens doesn't lecture like parents, able to say she make mistakes too. Friend-to friend.
- I look for some one who is always willing to answer questions, that is not a rascist or any other kind of bigot, some one who is into teaching for the sake of teaching (not just for the money). A teacher should be also someone you can relate to.
- A good teacher is not so set in her ways that she can't cope with a little change in the structure of the class. I like teachers who permit discussion and who can handle having their methods questioned by the students.
- An outstanding teacher is understanding, doesn't think so little of herself that she has to put a front on to gain respect, and she really tries to help the student.
- If they are open-minded and willing to listen to problems. To me a truly outstanding teacher is one that remembers back to when

he or she was a student in highschool and is compassionate with our problems.

- A teacher should be friendly and enjoy what she is teaching. A teacher that can do this and not be phony as a person is truly an outstanding teacher.

- In a teacher I look for integrity, personality, intelligence and patience. Of course if they look great, I don't mind.

- A good teacher must have huge amounts of faith and trust in her students—she must be very open-minded and able to discuss anything.

- Honesty, integrity, warmth, and love for students are the best features of any teacher. Such a person does not demand respect, but gets it. Such a person is original, imaginative and inventive.

- A teacher who likes his work, who cares about others and makes you feel comfortable in class. I like teachers that make you respect them so much so that you do alot of work for them, but afterwards realize that doing that work is helping you learn.

- Someone who really cares, someone who plans interesting things for your class to do or lets you do it on your own.

- He must be a human, understanding of the differences in people and truly caring. To be outstanding he must be a leader and then a teacher.

- A teacher should listen and learn from the students as well as teach. He is understanding, yet firm.

- I like a teacher who is honest and who truly cares about each of his students. I like a teacher who is *eager* to *teach* for only then will his pupils be eager to learn. I like a teacher who takes time.

- Someone who just doesn't come form 8–3:30 and puts in the minimum effort—But someone who really cares and wants to help you. Someone you can really talk to.

- Truthfulness, friendliness, understanding. One who has all these qualities and can make a person feel at ease—sort of drop the barrier. The same way because a teacher is a human being they souldn't have to put up a front.

QUESTION: *What do you most want from your teacher?*

STUDENT REPLIES

- Education without dictatorship. Thats getting a little far-out but what I mean is I wan't the facts and then I want to form my own ideas.

- I want to be in an intersting class, and the teacher is one who makes it that way—the students to, but the teacher has to do a lot of the framwork. I want a teacher to be more of a person, rather than a "teacher."

- I want them to be a resource to help me when I can't understand something, and to *advise* me (not tell me) about the best way to attack a problem.
- I would like a teacher to show me the way, not force me because that will turn me off to the whole learning trip, because it has. I would like teacher to act like they're human beings too not big college genius, who just teach little punks.
- I want him or her to understand me as a person and try to help me when I act as though I'm messed up. I would like her or him to see me as an adult and treat me like one and not a little kid!
- I want a friend. A person that I can go to and discuss the things that I have learned and to listen. I want suggestions not demands; help not hindrance.
- I feel that a teacher should be broad minded enough to at least talk to the student (if they want help), if they have a problem. This is what I want most from a teacher and a friend.
- A chance to think and feel what is real to me.
- I want understanding, patience, kindness, tenderness. And something I've never gotten from any other teachers. But I think those people are hard to find.
- The real thing I enjoy getting from a teacher is a person–person relationship instead of a teacher–student one.

QUESTION: *What are some things that bother you the most about teachers in general?*

STUDENT REPLIES

- I don't like the way most teachers insist on absolute silence in the room, and the way for some reason they don't think kids can learn if they work together. I despise re-admits and tardies and blue slips and off-campus permits and all that bullshit they use to keep their secure feeling of control over you.
- A lot of B.S. Some teacher don't express their own feelings. They tell students what they want to hear. I want to know how they as an individual feel. HONESTY.
- They are like seeing re-runs of old time movies for the 10 hundredth time.
- Some teachers tend to regard themselves as the All and Ever powerful Gods of Wisdom. No one is right but them. Other teachers seem to enjoy playing disciplinarian.
- They always stick to the books. They never explore new aspects of teaching. They don't care for the students. They think of us as a machine that they feed information into and expect us to accept everything without questions. They aren't even human beings, they're Gods who think they are infalable.

- How some teachers treat you as they treat everybody (just another student, another class). All they care about is giving you information on their subject and handing out homework. If you understand, fine, if you don't too bad, cause they don't have enough time to give to a student who needs help. All they care about is if you hand in your work so they can give you a grade.
- Teachers that think because they are older than me and because they are my teachers that they are all-knowing. They take on a smart or snippy attitude. Also teachers demand respect and demand that you look up to them. If they don't deserve it then they won't get it. Nothing is more sickening than a teacher that thinks he's better because he's older.
- Many teachers bring their problems from home to school, and take out their furstrations on the students. Others take the "Master–Slave" route and end up with an angry mob. Either way, they're in for trouble.
- There are teachers that like to scare their students and there are ones that like to feel as superior that they won't even answer questions. Then there are teachers that could give a damn about you, your feelings or even teaching.
- They are afraid to let their trueselves show through to the student. They are afraid to be honest and to trust becuase they don't want to risk the possibility of being let-down.
- They are structured to much. They have to do everything by the rules. They are boring because the structure is boring.
- They interpret materials for you and keep you from developing your own style and process of thinking. They also determine what we should learn in their course.
- Teachers who follow the patterns of others rather than their own.
- They're (many times) fake. They look down on me as not "old enough to understand" or "too young to speak or know my own mind." Many teachers put up a barrier between themselves and their students because they're afraid to let the kids see their own faults.
- Some teachers leave school as soon as the bell rings. They act as though they can't wait to leave. I would like to be able to come into a teachers room and talk to him not as a teacher but just as a friend!

4

Teachers' Struggles in
Becoming Therapeutic Persons

DIMENSIONS OF THE TEACHER AS A PERSON

Why is it, I've wondered, that teachers look everywhere but inside of themselves for answers to success in the classroom? They continually look for new methods of discipline and control, they frantically beg other teachers for their secrets, they attend summer workshops to hear the "authorities," hoping to steal some wisdom, and they ask for the latest books giving them the formula. Yet many of these same teachers resist facing themselves and coming to terms with themselves as persons. So many of us think there is some outside guru who can lead us down the path toward ecstasy. But in truth we can teach no further than we are as persons. We need to examine our basic motivations for entering teaching, become aware of our way of relating to learners, and get clear as to what personal needs are satisfied through our teaching. Discovering unknown dimensions of our selfhood is not a task that can ever be fully completed. The excitement of encountering fresh facets of our being is retarded when we become self-satisfied and content and want no more. To be sure, we need to consolidate our gains, and plateaus occur in personal growth as in all kinds of learning. But it is the *struggle* to work toward fuller self-realization that keeps us alive, not the reaching of a fixed condition.

THE STRUGGLE TO BECOME A THERAPEUTIC PERSON

Becoming a teacher who can make a difference in the lives of students involves being willing to struggle. This kind of person is the opposite of one who claims to be self-actualized, a completed, content, and perfectly secure person. The trouble with most of us is that we settle for what we already have—contentment—and we define our degree of happiness by an absence of conflict. I'm suggesting that true growth occurs only when we have the courage to recognize our limitations as persons and see the gap that exists between what we *are now*

55

and what we are *capable* of *becoming*. I suggest you reflect upon the last
five years, and ask yourself: "How have I changed during these past
five years? Am I satisfied with what I am becoming?" A further question: "What would I like my life to be five years hence? What kind of
person would I like to become? What goals do I want to strive for? And
what am I doing NOW with my life to make this vision a reality?"

BECOMING MORE DEMANDS RISK

While we all intellectually agree that there is always room for more
growth and "personal improvement," few will *really* believe and *act*
upon this. We go along hoping this "improvement" will somehow
automatically occur with the aging process. However there is no
growth without considerable risk—the risk of plunging ourselves into
unknown territory. Unfortunately, too many of us stay inert until we
are motivated by the pain of pressing problems to change our life
styles. The risk I speak of entails giving up some of the security of
known avenues and daring to venture down untraveled paths. The risk
can be leaving an unsatisfying career, or reaching out and creating
new relationships with people, or having the courage to withdraw
from a sick marriage, or moving to an exciting job without seniority.
There are no guarantees, and that is precisely what frightens us. We
balance the advantages of security versus growth. The person who has
a basic inner sense of security can risk further growth. The person
who is obsessed with security seldom plunges himself in risky situations where he might discover new facets of his experience.

BUT WHAT IF I HAVE NO PROBLEMS?

I can hear readers protesting, "But what if you are content, have
found yourself, and are perfectly satisfied with life? Must we always
be searching and risking? What if I've already found myself?" These
are the people that are *most* difficult to reach. If you are one of these
people, perhaps you ought to enjoy your contentment. But I think that
contentment is for cows, not people. Satisfaction with the status quo
seems to lead to stale living, not an exciting growing existence.

BECOMING AWARE

Awareness of self is a gradual, unfolding process. With limited
awareness comes only limited freedom. Then as you increase your
awareness, you also increase your possibilities for choosing a richer

life. This awareness is on several levels: awareness of your feelings, of your values and attitudes, of your basic motivations. The problem of many of us is closing ourselves to our experiences. We block out, filter, and distort much of our experience; we allow only those experiences to enter our awareness that are consistent with the image we have of ourselves. A sign of a growing person is his willingness to become more open to all experiences—being able to acknowledge, feel, and deal with a range of feeling experiences.

ALLOWING OURSELVES TO FEEL

A major portion of becoming is being willing to *unlearn* much of what you were taught and integrating new learnings in your life. We are taught the value of logic over emotions and cut off a significant part of living. We find it difficult to cry, feel tender, be compassionate, and unfortunately, we don't allow ourselves to need others. I submit that this denial of feeling impedes our effect upon our students. We deny feelings of anger, aggression, sexuality, hostility, and an entire range of "negative" and "unacceptable" feelings. Learning to own *all* our feelings, and integrate these feelings, is no easy task. It does take considerable new learning. Once you open yourselves to the range and depth of your emotions, you begin to learn that you can experience feelings, can trust them, and can enrich your life and relationships with people.

ACCEPTING OUR INCONSISTENCIES

Teachers make all sorts of impossible demands on themselves. We strive to be consistent beings. It is as though we highly value consistency within ourselves. In contrast, to me, it is growth to be able to tolerate your inconsistencies and even to learn how to enjoy them. Some illustrations and examples:

- Why do I need to be fair at all times? Perhaps I need to accept that much of the time I will be unfair. Is life *really* fair? Why do I need to be impartial? Why can I not accept my preferences? I know that I am going to be more attracted to some students than others, so why can't I learn to value my own discriminations? Why can't I accept that I am capable of loving and hating the same person? Why do I need to demand that I have room for only positive feelings toward those I love?

- Why do I make such demands on myself as always needing to be genuine? Why can't I accept that at times I will be phony? I can strive for greater realness, but it seems a mistake to expect myself to be real at all times.
- Can I be transparent, and also have my own private center that no one else knows? Can't I value transparency—making myself known to others when I so *choose* and to whom I choose, yet still valuing the dignity of a private domain?
- Why do I need to care for all of my students all the time? Isn't it more realistic to accept that at times I may really not care? If I can accept this attitude of not caring, then I've given up the released burden of living up to some external standard that I learned somewhere about the necessity of caring for all.

BEING ABLE TO DREAM AND FORM IDEALS

A beautiful aspect of being an adolescent is the ability to dream, to have ideals, and not to be soured with life. I think it's essential to dream—to imagine what you could or might have out of life and to be guided by a sense of idealism. Are you able to allow yourself to engage in fantasy about the *possible you,* the possible relationships you could have with others, and the possibilities of actively changing your environment?

I wonder what happens to us as we "mature" to cause us to lose most of our youthful ability to dream and fantasize the possible. There should be a way of recapturing our idealism. I suggest the way to regain lost idealism is by really putting ourselves in the world of the child and of the adolescent. In all of us resides that "child" and "rebellious adolescent," but most of us feel ashamed of those aspects of our being. To my mind, a mature person is one who is able to retain the spontaneity, freshness of appreciation, and curiosity of a child. Maslow (67) found his self-actualizing subjects were in many respects like children; they could appreciate reality in fresh, novel ways. If we can integrate the spirit of heightened emotional intensity, the idealism, and the "rebel" of our adolescent years, we can mature and at the same time not lose zest in life.

SELF-ACCEPTANCE:
THE BEGINNING OF PERSONAL CHANGE

We hear of the importance of accepting children as they are. We are told that unconditional acceptance of another is a sign of our respect for their personhood. If this "acceptance" implies taking a person for whatever he is, without any conditions or demands, then I do not favor this "acceptance." To me, *unconditional* acceptance signifies a lack of concern and respect. I hardly expect my loved ones to love me regardless of what I become or fail to become. I am fond of these words by Goethe: "If we take people as they are, we make them worse. If we treat them as if they were what they ought to be, we help them to become what they are capable of becoming."

Self-acceptance is the groundwork for the emergence of personal change. When I say "self-acceptance" I refer to our ability to be conscious of and open to our own characteristics. For example, if I am fifty pounds overweight, I doubt that I will lose any weight if I manage to convince myself that there are fatter people in the world, that my exterior being shouldn't be important, and that I could be even more overweight. As a prerequisite for change (losing weight), I first need to accept the reality of my overweight condition, and then decide what to do about this condition.

For most of us, self-acceptance is not an easy matter. We would like to deceive even ourselves (or particularly ourselves) in minimizing the ways we negate our own being. If I can learn to be open to my experience, and not filter this experience, I then have the power to make constructive changes in my personality. If I am basically an undisciplined soul, and I find myself moved to action only when someone else goads me out of my inertia, I need to accept this trait. I might decide that I *prefer* remaining undisciplined, or that self-discipline in whatever endeavor I might undertake is not worth the effort. But when I accept this characteristic as a reality of my being, the choice to change or not resides within me.

I have a great deal of respect for the men and women that I have encountered through Alcoholics Anonymous. Alcoholics will tell you that they were masterful at inventing justifications for why they got drunk. Everyone else around them recognized they were alcoholic *long* before the alcoholics could accept this knowledge themselves. Alcoholics are obsessed with self-deceptive gimmicks. Once they finally accept the fact that they *are* alcoholic, that they are allergic to alcohol, that they cannot drink in a controlled manner, then they begin to alter their life style radically.

TOLERATION OF AMBIGUITY

One measure of psychological well-being is the degree of ambiguity and uncertainty that can be tolerated. In my experience with teachers,

I have found that the majority have a low threshold for coping with ambiguity. Yet growth always entails leaving the familiar, the known, the tried, the secure, and plunging into uncharted territory. As a person builds his ego strength, he is developing more trust in himself. As he experiments with trusting his own intuitive processes, and as he more freely and less defensively moves with the spontaneous feelings, he begins to discover that he can trust these feelings. While his behavior is not always predictable, he is usually reliable. He comes to realize that his judgment is trustworthy. And this generates a greater toleration of the unknown. What teachers need to accept is that unless there is a certain amount of ambiguity, learning of any significance simply will not occur.

ON BEING UNIQUE

Teachers as a group seem to prefer conformity to uniqueness. We eschew the erratic, bizarre, weird side of ourselves almost as though we are afraid of emerging as a unique and distinctive self. Of course, there are some advantages to masking our special and idiosyncratic self—we go unnoticed and hence we are not singled out for negative criticism. Since teachers often squelch their own distinctiveness, they are vigilant in their search to nip in the bud any nonconformity their students might manifest. There is evidence for this in the preoccupation with student dress codes. Hair length, skirt length, shirt-tails worn outside of trousers, sideburns, hair styles and manner of speech are strictly controlled by the Establishment. The assumption is the same as in military life: if you control the troops in terms of dress and behavior, and you make them into uniformed, conforming humanoids, they will be easier to control.

I would be delighted to see teachers be truly large enough to permit uniqueness and diversity. Why can't teachers encourage pluralism? Why must each student march with the rest of his companions? Why is it that we are so frightened of the possibilities of allowing a range of diverse values? As a challenge, I recommend genuinely attempting to implement in your classroom practice the following thought by Henry David Thoreau:

> If a man does not keep pace with his companions, perhaps it is because he hears a different drummer. Let him step to the music which he hears, however measured or far away.

Educators have given lip-service to the ideal of education geared to the development of the unique individual for years. Isn't it about time that we begin to practice this in our classroom behavior?

LIVE UP TO YOUR OWN EXPECTATIONS

> I do my thing, and you do your thing. I am not in this world to live up to your expectations. And you are not in this world to live up to mine. You are you and I am I, and if by chance we find each other, it's beautiful. If not, it can't be helped. — Fritz Perls

This quotation is known as the Gestalt therapy prayer, written by the late Fritz Perls (29), founder of Gestalt therapy.

Many of us have lived our lives for so long by meeting the expectations of others that we have lost the sense of what we expect from and for ourselves. Our own identity is so blurred by attempting to conform to the standards of others that we find great difficulty in coming to terms with precisely what we value. Perls is misunderstood by many when he says "I do my thing and you do your thing." Some take this to mean that each of us ought to ignore others, and simply "do our thing." This would be irresponsible behavior. The meaning this prayer has for me is that I must find myself, that I alone must accept the responsibility for my behavior, that I must live by what I believe, and that I have a responsibility to become what I am capable of becoming. I want to be quick to add that my right to do my thing ends when I intrude on your rights as a person. If doing my thing happens to be riding my motorcycle on your freshly planted lawn, then I am interfering with you doing your thing of raising a beautiful lawn.

If all the teachers in a given school were to hang this Gestalt therapy prayer in the front of their rooms, and *sincerely try to put the spirit of these words into actual practice,* there would be a radical change in the quality of learning in that entire school. As things now stand, students know all too well that they *must* meet the expectations of their parents and teachers. All personal preferences, tastes, perceptions, and values are suppressed in favor of being appropriate and living the way the elders in their advanced wisdom deem best.

LEARNING TO BE SELFISH

Most of us have been taught that the proper way to live is by thinking of others before ourselves, and that it is much better to give to others than to receive from them. I see this attitude as an impediment to our growth as persons. One does not enable himself to give *genuinely* of himself to others by continually failing to recognize his own needs and working toward the satisfaction of these needs.

There are two styles of giving: from deprivation and from fulfillment. Consider the style of giving based upon deprivation. This is the person who does not recognize or meet his own human needs. Under the guise of being unselfish and altruistic, he consistently puts the other's needs before his own. He is self-sacrificing for the sake of others. But in reality, this "giving" is phony. The giver basks in the glory of being so noble by denying his own neediness. How virtuous to give continually and expect nothing in return for himself! Or does he expect no return for his investment? Does he not expect (perhaps demand) gratitude, appreciation, love, approval, respect from the person he so generously gives to? And is there not a sense of superiority in being the giver to others? Am I able to fill my emptiness by mustering to others' needs? Will not they make me feel as a valued person for "helping" them? Most of us have experienced receiving from the person who gives out of his lack of fulfillment. The teacher who is *totally* devoted to his students is a case in point. This teacher may arrive at school at 6:30 A.M. (two hours before classes begin), just in case some needy student may be seeking his counsel. He gives and gives unselfishly throughout the entire day—rarely even taking a coffee break for fear he may miss an opportunity to help a student. He remains at school until well after dinner time working in the service of others. He ignores his private life; in fact, he gives it up by encouraging students to feel free to call upon him at any time of the evening. It should be clear that this kind of teacher desperately *needs* his students to be in need of him—for it is his source of being, his very reason for existing. He must have dependent students so that he can feel of value.

The second style of giving is based upon giving to others out of personal fulfillment. This means that the individual is selfish enough to look after his own interests. He recognizes that he cannot be "on call" continually. He is able to enjoy his privacy. He can say no when he really feels like *not* giving. He is aware that if he attempts to play the role of the eternal giver, he will begin resenting the demands on his own time. Because he can be good to himself, take care of his own needs, and be truly selfish, he is able to give of himself out of his richness as a full person. Since he meets his needs, he can lose himself and be genuinely concerned with the fulfillment of others.

Learning to be selfish entails considerable un-learning. From early childhood, we are taught that we ought not to be selfish. Perhaps it would be good for us to attempt to live by the Biblical saying "Love thy neighbor as thyself." The idea is not to love our neighbor *more* than ourselves, but to love ourselves first and then work toward the goal of loving others in a similar way.

THE IMPORTANCE OF SELF-RESPECT

As teachers we are concerned that our students show us respect. While many teachers demand this respect simply because they are in a position of authority, it seems to me that the only kind of respect worth having is the kind that is genuinely given to us because we *earn* this respect by the way we are as persons.

Some of the clients I see in my office as a psychologist are people who have lost all self-esteem. These clients do not value themselves; they have lost their dignity as persons, and they hate what they have become. I think we cut away at our resources for recapturing lost self-respect if we blame outside circumstances for our present condition. How can you retain any measure of self-worth if you deny your own power to change your life? You need to accept that the power to alter your life condition resides within you, not outside of you with some set of circumstances. If you become painfully aware that you are entrapped in a dead-end job, that your marriage produces little joy but much frustration, that you find yourself growing stale, that you feel empty most of the time, that life has lost any substantial meaning, then perhaps you should consider that you have in life what you're willing to settle for. Could it just be that you do have what you bargain for? What you have deserved? What you have chosen? If you are continually miserable in your relationships with others and in your present way of being, then you must *want* what you have, or else you would be doing something to alter your life style.

The beginning of earning genuine self-respect occurs when you accept personal responsibility for your own living. As each of us makes changes in his life, based upon consciousness and self-awareness, he increases his feelings of personal power and dignity. No longer are we pawns of an external fate, but we each have accepted our capacity to make choices and transcend external barriers to internally derived goals.

THE ABILITY TO LOVE AND BE LOVED

I have been puzzled why in most states teachers are not issued teaching credentials until they successfully complete a course in audiovisual methods and materials, while I know of no state that requires the applicant to produce any evidence that he has the capacity to love or care about others, that he is a loving person, or that he has ever felt loved by anybody. I assume that state boards deem it more important that a teacher know how to thread a film projector than be the kind of person that can relate to children with love.

Volumes have been dedicated to the ability to love and be loved, and my intent is not to add still another book on the subject. My purpose is to call attention to the relevance of love in the personal and professional life of a teacher. As I observe teachers in their classrooms, I often have the feeling that the teacher is functioning more like an efficient machine than an open, caring human. I've seen teachers impersonally respond to their students as objects—objects to be controlled, informed, or in some other way to be manipulated. If a teacher is to touch and affect his students' lives significantly, and if he is to do more than simply teach a subject *to* them, he must be capable of loving (respecting and caring for them as individuals worthy of dignity). Here I am not proposing that he love *all* students at *all* times. What I refer to is his capacity to demonstrate through his classroom behavior his respect for students as persons. Before this concern can be shown to students, the teacher must first feel self-respect and self-love, and he must possess a sense of dignity; in short, he must care about himself.

In *The Art of Loving* (58), Erich Fromm mentions four basic elements common to all forms of love: *care, responsibility, respect,* and *knowledge*. *Care* implies an active concern for the life of the loved one. *Responsibility* signifies that we choose to be responsive to the needs of the person we love. *Respect* implies an absence of exploitation and desire for the growth and well-being of the person we love. *Knowledge* means that without knowing the person, love is not possible. A genuine act of love toward students is in giving them what they have a right to—their own responsibility for themselves and their lives. To do so is to affirm their dignity as persons.

SEARCHING FOR MEANING IN LIFE

A dimension of everyone's life is the quest for meaning and purpose. Without a sense of purpose, life is empty. Sometimes we become so involved in performing our functions as teachers, mothers, fathers, friends, or whatever, that we fail to ask ourselves what is the purpose behind our existence. Perhaps it is necessary to endure extreme deprivation to come to terms with the existential questions: Why am I living? What does it all mean? So what? What do I really value? Viktor Frankl describes a lucid account of a man's struggle to find a "why" for living when one is in an extreme condition of aloneness—a concentration camp. In his book *Man's Search for Meaning* (57), he shows us how we can endure almost any "how" if we discover a "why" for our existence.

Some questions we might ask ourselves in the attempt to clarify the nature of personal meaning in life are:

1. What are the sources of value in my life?
2. Do I have a belief in religion? If so, how does this influence my decisions? How does it affect my behavior? How and why did I come to believe what I believe?
3. Why do I choose to remain living? What gives my life any direction? How much zest do I have for living? Am I really living or merely existing?
4. Where am I going? What kinds of goals am I working toward? What do I want to be remembered for when I die?
5. If life seems to be a void, where do I begin to discover ways of finding substance?
6. Have I challenged the values I live by or have I merely unconsciously and automatically accepted values that were taught to me?

ACCEPTANCE OF OUR ALONENESS

The existentialists believe that man is ultimately alone. Each of us comes into this world alone and we leave the world alone. For many this thought is terrifying. Running into activity, continually surrounding ourselves by friends, habitually and excessively using alcohol and drugs, burying ourselves in either work or play—all are ways we can attempt escape from the experience of being alone.

We have other ways of denying our aloneness. One is religion. While religion can be a source of strength and a significant factor in helping you find meaning in life, it can also be based upon neurotic needs. If you submit your entire being to a church, and you let that church dictate the standards for your living, then you might not feel as alone in the world. Guarantees are provided for the "true believer." By living by others' precepts you need not endure the anxiety of choosing your own way in life. It can be a most lonely experience to cope with existing when you look within and formulate your own ethics based upon your own experience and judgment.

There is a difference between *aloneness* (which can give us a sense of power and help us discover the core of our being) and being *lonely*. We need solitude to pull back from the confusion of living with others. In alone moments you can center on who you are, what you stand for, what life means, what you want to give to life and what you want from it. In solitude you can begin to sort out values that have been imposed upon you from values that have their source within your very being. Alone time can be helpful in any relationship. If married persons separated even for a week-end and each went on a private retreat, each might bring back a renewed basis for the relationship.

Moustakas has written of the value of solitude in man's life. He sees solitude as man's organic tie to himself and to the universe. Alone time is an opportunity to renew contact with ourselves, to discover who we are; it is an opportunity to break through static patterns that prevent our rich encounter with life. Moustakas, in his book *Individuality and Encounter*, makes the point that solitude of itself is often not enough to cause us to break new ground; the feeling of anguish, of being alienated and frustrated is needed. He says,

> Often it is necessary that the person feel the anguish of loneliness, that he feel cut off from the sources of genuine life, that he feel the agony of loss of human meaning, and that he know the tragic separation from his own self. It is important that the person feel the emptiness of existence all the way—and that the individual recognize the basic loneliness of separateness, and let these feelings stand (85, p. 20).

DISCLOSURE OF SELF

Sidney Jourard is a psychologist who has devoted much of his professional life to researching and thinking about disclosure of self as a key to well-being. His book *The Transparent Self* (62) is one I recommend for every educator or professional who deals with people.

Most of us have learned to be guarded. We wear armor when it is not appropriate. Each of us peeks out at the other from behind chinks in this iron suit. It is as though we fear that if we disclose aspects of our being to a person we are in relationship with, this person will now have a weapon with which to bludgeon us. We see the others as vicious sharks who are out to eat us alive.

Jourard maintains that it is through disclosure of self to others that we grow and gain in self-awareness. To hide our real selves chronically results in sickness. He describes "sickening roles" that we play so the social system will work. The trouble is that we forget that it is a *person* who is playing a role. And so we hide ourselves from our students behind our "teacher mask," and they present us with their "student masks." There is no real person-to-person meeting in these relationships. The tragedy here is that we become alienated from our own selves as well as from others in our staying behind fixed roles. It is true that the way we come to know ourselves is by disclosing ourselves to other persons.

I suggest the teacher can use Jourard's concept of the "psychotherapist as exampler" for his new role. "He is a guide to more expanding, fulfilled, and fulfilling ways to experience life as a person. . . . He has a robust interest in his own fulfillment and pursues this, in part, by helping others to fulfill themselves. . . . He experiments with *his* existence, seeking ways that generate maximum enlightenment, freedom, and love" (62, p. 157). This is a bold and exciting model for the "new teacher," and I feel convinced that this is one of the surest ways of touching our students deeply—by living what we teach and by being an example of a human being in struggle.

LEARNING TO LIVE IN THE *NOW*

One of the contributions of Gestalt therapy is the emphasis upon the here-and-now—not the past and not the future. We avoid experiencing the full awareness of the present moment when we get hung up on what we *might* have been or done. Preoccupation with what will be (the future) is another way of avoiding the intensity of the here-and-now.

Perls, in *Gestalt Therapy Verbatim* (29), makes the point that we hang on to our past in order to justify our unwillingness to grow. For Perls maturity means "taking responsibility for your life—being on your own." His formulation is that "maturing is the transcendence from environmental support to self-support." Perls feels that we live only five to fifteen percent of our potential, because:

> We live in clichés. We live in patterned behavior. We are playing the same roles over and over again. So if you find out how you prevent yourself from growing, from using your potential, you have a way of increasing this, making life richer, making you more and more capable of mobilizing yourself. And our potential is based upon a very peculiar attitude: to live and review every second afresh (29, p. 29).

Learning to live for the *now*, and learning to take responsibility for what we are now, is a key to getting ourselves unstuck from sterile, deadening patterns that lock us into the status quo. As Perls mentions, the trouble with most of us is we get caught up in a whirl by making all sorts of resolutions of what our future will be like or rationalizing our present zombie-like state by our past. We would rather do anything than become conscious of how we prevent ourselves from being fully alive, and work through the impasse. I like the way Perls puts it: "We'd rather manipulate others for support than learn to stand on our own feet and to wipe our own ass" (29, p. 39).

SUMMARY: BECOMING YOUR OWN PERSON

The central theme of this chapter has been that the most important aspect the teacher has to offer is *himself as a person*. Subject matter competency and knowledge of modern teaching techniques are secondary to the *kind of human being the teacher is*. In concluding, let me stress the importance of becoming your own person. You must work through parental influences and substitute your own internal values for outside values (values of parents and parent substitutes). In short, the person who becomes his own person is the one who lives primarily by his inner standards and by his own approval, rather than one who lives chiefly by the standards of others and the approval and acceptance of others.

How do we emerge into this separate and unique kind of person? How are we able to overcome our past conditioning? Are we able to psychologically kill off the influence of our parents and their substitutes? At birth the first separation occurs—the physical separation of the cutting of the umbilical cord. Later comes the necessity for a kind of psychological cutting off from parents. This latter separation is not automatic, and it comes only through the deliberate choice of the person. At a very early age, the child fights for his independence. He struggles to get free. He goes through negativistic stages and boldly attempts to assert his autonomy. Perhaps how the parents react at this time has a significant impact on how the child will succeed in growing into adulthood. The parents can retard the child's development by not letting go. For many parents, watching their children mature is a threat. They are losing their babies. It forces the parents to face the realization that they too are getting older. These parents frequently need their children to be carbon copies of themselves. They mold, impose their standards, and insist upon blind compliance to their standards.

The tragedy of this situation is that many of these children become psychological cripples. They learn to depend upon their parents for direction in life. These children are learning a lesson—I must be feeble and incompetent, or else why would my parents make all of my decisions? It becomes easier simply to accept parental standards than to attempt to develop a personal system of values. Such children learn to depend upon their parents for help in all areas of decision making: selection of clothes, hair styles, choice of friends, etc. Since the child basically mistrusts himself as a decision maker, he avoids making choices as often as possible. There are advantages to this: the comfort of being taken care of, the security similar to that of being housed and protected in the womb, the easing of the burden of personal responsibility. But the price he pays for this security is costly indeed; he sells his soul, he deprives himself of his dignity and sense of self-worth, he allows himself to remain at an infantile level of dependence upon others, he surrenders his autonomy, and thus he deprives himself of the basis necessary for becoming an individual person.

What are the alternatives? We can dare to risk growth. We can risk ourselves by leaving the security of home and charting our own course in life. To do this means that we have to be willing to give up our parents' approval, which also implies a psychological death of our parents. This does not mean that we reject all of our parental teaching, but it does mean that we have challenged the values our parents have offered us. We dare to search within ourselves for our own sense of direction. Even though our choices may be wrong, and though we are never sure of our decisions, we dare to trust ourselves enough to act upon choices that seem right to us. This kind of living calls for learning how to make decisions and use our freedom. Every choice we make opens up the possibilities for further choice. But with this freedom comes the awesome weight of responsibility. This is precisely the reason many attempt to "escape from freedom" as Erich Fromm has so clearly described.* When we become aware of the impact of this responsibility it generates feelings of anxiety. Anxiety in this sense can be very healthy. It is not anxiety per se that is harmful, but our reaction to this anxiety that is the crucial determinant. It takes genuine courage to live with the anxiety that comes with the awareness that we *must* take personal responsibility for our own lives and accept the fact that we are largely what we have chosen to become. We have the potential to shape our own destiny, but whether we use this capacity for choice is another matter.

---

* See Erich Fromm, *Escape from Freedom*, New York: Holt, Rinehart & Winston, 1941.

In order to open ourselves to the possibility of using our freedom, we must first become aware of the nature of parental influences described earlier. We must first have an awareness of *how* our values have been determined by our parents (and parental substitutes), and then we can make a decision as to whether or not we will allow their influences to have an impact upon our present behavior. We can choose to risk being ourselves only if we are willing to relinquish the total acceptance of our parents. Then we must look within and search our own souls for the values that have meaning to us. Sometimes these internally-derived standards will differ sharply from some of our outer-directed values. But it seems to me that the only true basis for becoming a unique person is the looking within and asking of ourselves how we ought to live and forming our own guidelines. Living in this style is not comfortable; and there are no guarantees. In fact, the person who is his own person can be guaranteed his fair share of loneliness, rejection by others, anxiety, doubt, and even guilt. With consciousness we can learn to tolerate ambiguity. We can acquire the ability to live life without guarantees and without certain rewards.

The person who is working at his own emergence as a person is one who is struggling with overcoming the tendency for other-directedness. For many people, all the cues for behaving, thinking, and feeling are oriented outside of the self. Some look consistently to others for how they *ought* to live, *ought* to feel, *ought* to value, *ought* to think, and *ought* to behave. They are victims of others' values. Part of this relates to the need to be accepted and approved by everyone. It is as though the person is saying, "If I become what you expect me to become, then you will like me, and I will feel accepted." The core of this problem is that this kind of person is frustrated because of the impossibility of pleasing everyone. Also, since his behavior is largely an attempt to meet expectations of others, he loses his own ability to know what he expects of himself. He plays so many roles that he becomes confused. He wears many maks and is continually changing these masks to fit the situations. This shifting of values gets him into real trouble because it eventually leads to an alienation from himself.

The becoming that has been described here is not something we achieve once and for all. It is a process characterized by considerable struggle from moment to moment. We never "arrive" as the Finished Person; rather it is the *struggle to become more* that keeps us feeling alive.

5

Personal Growth for Teachers in Encounter Groups

One of the most powerful instruments for change for teachers is the encounter group. Through the vehicle of group procedures, teachers can make significant gains in personal and professional growth; so that they are able to enhance their relationships with other people and so that they are able to become more self-confident, which allows them to experiment and modify their styles as classroom teachers.

In the encounter groups to be discussed, we rarely talk about teaching and learning issues or educational matters. Instead, these groups take a more personal direction where the participants explore the quality of their human relationships, their marriages, their life styles, their deepest values, and their hang-ups that obstruct their growth toward the kinds of persons they wish they could be. The teachers in these intensive groups encounter themselves and others in ways that are often new for them. Since the groups are primarily experimental, members encounter feelings and learn to express these feelings. They begin to learn that relying upon intellect and logic is not enough. In short, they experience a wider dimension of themselves as persons.

Teachers who have been in these encounter groups have consistently reported that both they and their students notice changes in the way they relate to their classes. Teachers become less afraid of their students, less fearful of experimenting with a freer, more student-centered class, less frightened of losing their "professional dignity," and much more open, warm, trusting, and direct. Teachers become less compulsive about covering required ground and more concerned with creating a climate where the teacher and the students can have real exchanges of ideas and feelings. In essence, as teachers become more real, more human and humane, more personable, they tend to become therapeutic change agents for their students.

I struggle when I attempt to write or speak about encounter groups. It is difficult to convey accurately what these groups are really like, what occurs, and what participants experience. What I have tried to do is raise questions that I am frequently asked about groups and then answer them. An account that omitted the participants' views would be incomplete, so a section is devoted to statements from a variety of participants on how they experienced the group, what changes it made in them, and the effects of the experience in their daily lives.

SOME BACKGROUND

In this chapter I want to share with you one of the most exciting and rewarding of my current professional endeavors. During the past several years I have offered special workshop-type courses which were essentially encounter groups for teachers and people in related fields. These courses were a part of the extension programs at California State Polytechnic University at Pomona, the University of California at Riverside, and California State University at Fullerton. In my current work at the Interdisciplinary Center at California State University at Fullerton, working with students in personal growth groups and training people to become group leaders are my primary functions.

Some of names of these courses that were offered through the extension programs were "Human Relations for Teachers," "Encounter for Teachers," "Group Process and Leadership," and "Personal and Professional Problems of Teachers." The theme of the courses is basically that of creating a climate where each member is free to be himself and is given permission to express his feelings both verbally and nonverbally. A major aim of the group experience is for each individual to become aware of his individual life style and gain awareness of the impact of his person upon other persons. In these group courses, the emphasis is upon dealing with our fears of ourselves and others, working through barriers to trust, risking ourselves in the presence of others, growing toward openness and authenticity, and giving and receiving feedback.

I have experimented with a variety of formats, including weekly three-hour group sessions, three or four all-day groups, two all-day Saturday and Sunday groups, overnight marathon sessions which generally begin Friday evening and go continuously until Saturday afternoon for a total of twenty hours, a series of two of these overnight marathons with follow-up sessions, and three-day live-in groups in a mountain setting. Currently most of my groups meet at a place I have in the mountains of Idyllwild for a three-day period during which the participants live together. Generally we have at least four working sessions which last five hours each. We then meet again for a second week-end session of twenty hours a couple of weeks later. In addition to the group working time of almost fifty hours, members are given free time for personal meditation, walks in the woods, forming small informal groups, and play and relaxation. After the two separate weekend encounter workshops, at least one follow-up session is scheduled to share experiences of what the group meant, how we are using new learnings, problems in applying what we learned in group to the outside world, and to provide reinforcement of changes in our relationships.

AN OVERVIEW OF THE PROCESS AND DEVELOPMENT OF A GROUP

While each group is unique in terms of process, problems explored, dynamics, and outcomes, there have been some observable trends in most of the teacher groups with which I have worked during the past several years. Here is a general picture of the development of a group from the time when twenty people are strangers to the end of the group's history when they have formed intimate relationships.

Before the initial session, the members usually decide to "drop out" of the group. Many express ambivalent feelings: "I want to be a part of the encounter group, but I'm scared!" It is not at all unusual for people to develop a range of psychosomatic complaints, and the anxiety level rises as the time for the initial meeting approaches. When the time finally comes, participants generally wait in anticipation for something to happen—and most of the talk is on the surface only. One of the first things I ask the participants to do is to state how they feel now, what they came expecting, what they most want from this experience, and what their greatest fears are at the moment.

Typical comments voiced during this initial go-around are:

- "I'm not sure what to expect. I came partly out of curiosity, and partly because I'm not satisfied with what I am now. I want more out of life, and I hope I can find some direction here."
- "I'd like to be less inhibited. I feel that I always need to please everyone. Will you all like me, accept me, and approve of me? This is what I hope to change in this group."
- "Somehow my life seems stale. My relationships with my students seem lacking, but I'm not sure what to do about it."
- "I'd like to get feedback on how I come across to people. If I can be honest and open up in here, then I can get your honest reactions to me."
- "Do I wish I could trust people? I'm very timid about trusting

anyone's feelings toward me. I'd like to find out if I want to trust
you people."

- "It's difficult for me to share my feelings. People tell me that all
  they get from me is my intellect. I want to learn how to recognize
  my feelings, and hopefully be able to share them."
- "My greatest fear is that I will sit here the entire time and not get
  involved . . . that I will be a detached observer."
- "My fantasy is that if I really open up that I will discover ugly stuff
  in me, and that would be hard to take. What if I am nothing?"
- "I'm afraid that if I reach out, that you will reject me. You might
  ignore me, laugh at me, call me a fool, or throw me out of the
  group."
- "Since I've never been to one of these encounter things before, I
  don't know what to expect, but I feel perfectly calm. I'll let what
  happens, happen!"
- "I really don't think I have any major problems. But I'd like to
  learn how to listen better, and how to help others."
- "I'd like to get the anger out of my system that I feel over my recent
  divorce. Somehow I'm stuck with all sorts of feelings that I've
  never really worked through."
- "I expect to have communication with others in here that is real—
  not like the stuff that goes on in the teachers' lounge. I want to
  be honest with you, and I want your honesty."

After each of us expresses our expectations, desires, and fears, there
is usually a period of testing out each other. Instead of plunging into
deep waters, there is more of a tendency to wade in shallow waters
for a time. Our walls are still standing. We haven't yet allowed others
to see beneath the self that we present in everyday life. Eventually
somebody challenges the group for staying on a superficial level. The
challenger receives a challenge back from hostile members. How dare
this person confront us! Risk taking begins, and this seems to change
the level of a group. One person reaches out and asks for something,
or he discloses something about himself that takes courage, or he
directly confronts a person with real feelings, or in some other way
people begin to risk. In risking, the trust among the members deepens.
As this trust and concern emerge, members share experiences they
usually keep private. There is identification when the members see
much of themselves in others. For years we think we are alone with
our feelings, and now we begin to discover that we have the same
struggles as others in this room. Genuine closeness is emerging, a sense
of community is developing. The members now engage in greater
degrees of self-disclosure and sharing. Members reach out to other

members with concern, warmth, love, and acceptance. Continuous feedback is an integral part of this process. As we disclose our problems, struggles, desires, fears, goals, and other personal feelings, we receive feedback from the group that can be very useful to us in several ways. From this feedback we gain more awareness of our life style and how our behavior affects others. Also, we have the chance to experiment with new behavior to discover more satisfying ways of meeting our needs.

With the formation of a caring community, negative feelings can be owned and expressed. Persons in the group experience a freedom to feel as they do, and not to apologize for the feelings. Members show a greater willingness to accept personal responsibility for their own feelings and actions, instead of burdening themselves with guilt for making others feel a certain way.

An important aspect of group process is the active involvement among the members. I believe in sharing the leadership roles. In a group of twenty, there are many people who can be of real value to each other. At various times, there are twenty group leaders. I use this phenomenon of willingness of members to respond actively to each other as one index of an effective group.

As the group works through various phases, there is a movement toward greater realness and basic honesty. Involvement intensifies; risk taking increases: people become willing to face feelings they have long denied; they struggle to work through these feelings. We become clearer with ourselves, and we see barriers to our own becoming as a person. Decisions on important matters begin to be made. Thus, twenty strangers use the group experience itself as a vehicle for growth —a human laboratory where new behavior can be tried. Here is a place where attitudes can be examined, where values which have been unchallenged can stand the test of confrontation, and where we can get more closely in touch with our deepest experiences.

KEY THEMES EXPLORED IN THE INTENSIVE GROUP SESSIONS

While no two groups are the same, I have found that there are some common themes—general human concerns, struggles, conflicts, and experiences—which are often brought out in a group and explored in depth. What follows is a discussion of some of the areas of human experience that we usually work on with intensity in these week-end encounter sessions.

LONELINESS

A common theme in most groups is learning how to understand and live with loneliness. We all want and need other people. But from the existential viewpoint, loneliness is a universal characteristic of man. Ultimately we are alone. With this loneliness comes a sense of power at times. To find ourselves we need solitude. Time alone is not a luxury, but a necessity. It is too common that in groups members have confessed that they fear being alone. They tell of the need to always be around people, to have radios blasting, or to be occupied all the time. For some, being alone is a threat to self. The fear that if we are alone then we will have to come to grips with our emptiness is a grave fear for many. Clark Moustakas has devoted an entire volume to loneliness (72). As he indicates, there are many experiences which we must bear alone—childbirth, the death of a loved one, and ultimately our own death.

In the personal growth groups I frequently have the participants spend some time alone to reflect on what they are experiencing. A technique to foster feelings of loneliness is the use of mild hypnosis. Each person is asked to let his body relax while he thinks of a scene where he once found himself alone. Through suggestion the participants are led into fantasy and relive some earlier childhood (or adolescent) experience where they were totally alone. After the experience of this loneliness, each person is asked to tell what he experiences. The aim here is to help us learn to use loneliness creatively, not to avoid it. The purpose is also to teach us how we can overcome loneliness by reaching out to other people.

SEARCH FOR FATHER AND MOTHER

In reflecting upon the marathons in which I was involved, I cannot remember many groups that did not deal with mother and father figures. A few groups revolved around dealing with fathers. Most of us have unfinished business with our parents. There are all kinds of parents to be dealt with: the father who never had time for his children, the cold mother, the seductive mother, the father who left his family, the mother who didn't want her children, the mother unable to show her affection, the father who beat his kids, etc. In most of us, there are strong feelings toward our fathers and mothers which remain sealed off from us. Feelings of love, hate, anger, rejection, and guilt are just a few emotions which are frequently brought to the fore. I have found that when one participant begins to "talk to his father," others in the group begin to feel these same feelings. This becomes somewhat contagious. One method used to bring out these feelings is to have the members talk to an empty chair. The person doesn't know what he will say as he approaches the chair, but when he stands before the chair he is often amazed at the emotional flow toward a parent. A number of times I have had clients tell me that as a result of the practice and the release of talking to the chair, they were finally "able to have a dialogue with their problem parent—and for the first time in their lives, they were able to tell their feelings directly to that parent.

Role playing and psychodrama are also of value in assisting us in dealing with our parents. In one group I recall a middle-aged woman talking about her depression, her hate for her husband, her inability to find any joy in life, and her feelings of hopelessness. This sparked a young lady in the group. "That's my mother!" Immediately this young girl began attacking the "mother," and the "mother" began relating to the "daughter." This type of spontaneous role playing can be significant in recognizing some of our buried emotional life. In order to become our own persons, it is a must that we learn how to cope with our parents. We need to come into contact with what we wanted (and still want) from them, how they have failed us, how much we miss them, how we feel toward them, how we want their approval and love; and we need to learn that even though we cannot change our parents or our past with them, we can change our present attitudes and relationships with them.

REJECTION

We commonly hear people in these groups talk about their fears of being rejected. This feeling of rejection might well have its roots in childhood experiences with our parents. Now the person avoids intimacy with others because he doesn't want to suffer similar rejection again. It's as though he is saying, "If my parents didn't love me, then who can?" By isolation and withdrawal the person protects himself from hurt, but he pays the price in terms of alienation and loneliness. During the group, the participants are encouraged to talk about what the rejection feels like and what will happen if they dare to trust others with their feelings. Many who want to overcome their fears of rejection try again and reach out. Instead of being pushed away, they usually find themselves loved and accepted by the group. But this acceptance is not unconditional. There are some people who present themselves in such a way as to get rejected by others. Some are simply obnoxious, and then when the group excludes them they reply, "See,

I'm right—nobody loves me!" There is only one difference here. Perhaps for the first time in his life, he knows *why* he is being rejected. If the group will be honest with him, they can give him feedback that he can choose to use. At least now he is able to change his attitudes and behavior that lead to rejection.

ALIENATION

A popular term today is *alienation,* feelings of being cut off from ourselves, from others, or from nature. This feeling of alienation is often explored during the intensive enounter sessions. There is the feeling that we are alone and that we cannot feel a part of anything. The experience of being on the periphery of human activity and never really involved with people is a manifestation of this separation from self and others. All of us need to be loved and accepted, to feel a sense of relationship with other beings, to have a sense of relatedness and rootedness. Our urban mechanized society augments feelings of alienation. We live in congested cities, separated from nature. People are viewed as objects to be manipulated. There is a hurry about the routine of our daily lives. There is little that we see in nature or in others to which we can relate meaningfully. The nature of the basic encounter group itself is a positive force in the direction of overcoming this sense of alienation.

There are concerned people around us to whom we can choose to relate, to whom we can reach out, whom we can trust, and to whom we can reveal ourselves. Within this intensive group experience the potential for forming bonds with other human beings exists. But we must make the choice; we must reach out for these people. You might be thinking aloud, "Fine, this is great for the few hours that I am involved in the group, but what about when I return to the cold real world outside?" One of the significant learnings emerging from the group experience is that we can, if we choose to and if we have the courage to, carry our behavior outside to the real world. If people are lovable in the group we can find the same kind of people outside of the group. Human needs are the same everywhere. But it does call for effort and a conscious decision on our part.

ANXIETY

There is a healthy anxiety that is a part of the human condition. This normal anxiety is a product of our acceptance of our internal freedom. There is also neurotic anxiety that can cripple us. This kind of noncreative anxiety can grow out of a number of sources: competition with others, fear of failure, rejection, feelings of inferiority, poor self-concept, real or imagined lacks, etc. In general, most of the themes dealt with in therapy (individual and groups) relate to anxiety. Anxiety is a motivational force. It can serve as a warning signal that all is not well, and it can direct our efforts along constructive channels.

By dealing with feelings that produce anxiety, we lessen the anxiety itself. It is a mistake to think of eliminating all anxiety. Rather we should think in terms of learning how to live constructively with anxiety; that is, converting neurotic anxiety into healthy anxiety. Finally, a most important thing to learn about anxiety is that we need to have courage to function with anxiety. If we are living a life with purpose, there is bound to be the anxiety that springs from our awareness that it is we who are responsible for our lives.

FREEDOM

Learning how to be free is a central theme of most personal growth groups. The nature of this freedom has been described by writers such as Frankl, May, Fromm, and Rogers. This is not the place to discuss at length the nature of freedom. The purposes of groups are to help people become free agents, to encourage them to use their freedom constructively, to augment self-awareness that forms the basis of choice, and to have them recognize the consequences of being a free person.

At marathons one can witness prisoners who are unfree and shackled. There are prisoners who are bound to their past, prisoners in a poor marriage, those stuck in unsatisfying jobs, people who are prisoners to their parents, those who are chained by guilt feelings, those who dare not make a decision because they do not trust themselves, people who are victims of leading a life by others' expectations, those bound to an authoritarian religion, to mention just a few forms of lack of freedom. The central thrust of a group experience is to provide the type of atmosphere where the person is able to become aware of how and in what ways he is a prisoner. In this way, he is in a position to choose to free himself of this determinism.

DEATH

Not too many people are able to take their eventual death seriously. We are a culture that denies the reality of death. Our terminology relating to death is a sign of how we deny this reality. In the intensive group how we feel about our own death is sometimes explored. More frequently death is explored through a participant's dealing with the death of a loved one.

Feelings of guilt over causing the death of a parent, our death wishes toward them and the corresponding guilt, are not uncommon topics. Such feelings need to be released, expressed, and explored. We need to learn that our fantasies (even death wishes) are not powerful enough to cause actual death. Even after we understand this intellectually, the feelings of guilt may persist and it may take time to learn how to resolve these feelings of guilt.

Existentialists contend that death is a relevant variable—that in order to develop a rich life with meaning, we must accept the reality of our eventual nonbeing. To take death seriously can result in marked anxiety. But it is the confrontation with our own nonbeing that jars us into making the most of this present moment. This realization helps us realize our potential.

I remember a particular marathon where one man was talking about his desire to commit suicide. Only his religion (fear of going to hell) and his cowardice kept him from killing himself. In essence, however, he was living a "dead life." No joy, fulfillment, dreams, happiness were a part of him. His potential as a person was withered. He was asked to assume a prone position on the floor and "play dead" while others spoke about him. He was asked eventually to fantasize his own funeral—who would be there, what they would say, and so on. This method can be useful in helping a person confront his dead existence; at this point he is in a better position to choose to continue this negative existance or choose to live a life with some purpose.

MEANING IN LIFE

Related to the treatment of death is the issue of finding a meaning that makes life worth living. There are some very common questions raised in the groups being described such as: Why am I here? What do I want from my life? Is there any purpose in living? Is my work giving me a meaning in my life? Is religion a source of meaning? Does God have any meaning in my life? Is my family a source of meaning? What values are mine and what values are worth living for? What goals am I striving toward? What can I do to find a why for living? These and similar questions are often raised either directly or indirectly. The reader who wants a further account of the search for meaning in life is referred to Frankl's work. In one book (57) he shows dramatically how it is possible to find a *why* for living even in an extreme situation of deprivation.

In short, the issue of what we want from life and what we want to give to life is subject matter for these sessions. The aim is to provide a beginning for participants to search themselves honestly so that they can clarify their real values. Too often we find ourselves living by the values of society, our parents, a church, an organization—by all kinds of other-generated values. The real task is to learn how to create our own values—values that will give us a sense of substance, a sense of uniqueness and individuality, and a source for building meaning into our lives. I'm not suggesting that this search for inner values and the quest for meaning is established as a result of a few group experiences. Perhaps all that can be hoped for is that the process is encouraged and initiated by these sessions. The search for meaning is a life-long quest.

LEARNING TO LOVE AND TRUST

Most of the groups I have been involved with dealt largely with learning how to love and give trust. First, participants need to learn how to trust in themselves, and they must learn that self-love is a prerequisite for learning how to care for, be genuinely interested in, and actually love others. People need to develop an inner confidence in their own ability to live by their own, not others', wishes. Some have been so concerned with gaining the pseudo-love of others that they have never really felt this sense of trust in self. Because of this failure to trust in themselves to be the masters of their lives, these people have the feeling that others cannot be relied upon—that if you trust your feelings to others they will somehow hurt you.

DEALING WITH SEXUALITY

Another theme of encounter groups is our feelings about sexuality. In our culture many areas are taboo—homosexual feelings, incestual feelings, etc. The fact is that often these unresolved feelings in us block our relationships with members of both sexes. The typical man in our culture admits that it is not manly to cry, to feel tenderness, and to have "feminine" feelings. His "tender side" must be repressed, for this part of him is not congruent with his view of the "virile man." In the intensive group experience these feelings are commonly explored. One learns to express feelings that he has kept hidden. He learns to be less frightened of these feelings. The distinction between possessing sexual feelings and acting upon these feelings is also learned.

As children we learned that there are some feelings that are "bad"—such as anger and sexuality. Children are able to freely express real hatred and anger toward those who frustrate them. Soon this child learns that his anger is not an acceptable part of him. Others won't be pleased with him when he becomes angry. This anger becomes repressed, and as a result we begin to lose our ability to *feel* anger. Sexual feelings are repressed in the same way.

Since these feelings have been so successfully repressed by many, much of what occurs in groups is an unlearning. For many of the participants, they have been unaware of these feelings and actively cut them out of conscious experience for a lifetime. The group cannot change this immediately. What can happen is that these feelings are brought to awareness and allowed expression. A person learns that he is not evil for hating those he loves at times. We learn that our sexual feelings are not abnormal, and that they will not destroy us or others if we allow them into awareness. This is another example of learning how to trust ourselves and our own experiencing.

THE RISKS INVOLVED

Are there some risks and dangers involved in participating in encounter sessions? Yes. Committing yourself to really working in a group is both risky and frightening. What we need to clarify are these questions: Are the possible advantages of this experience worth the risks involved? Are you willing to pay a price for personal growth?

What we've found is that as people become more fully aware of sickening roles and relationships that obstruct personal growth, it almost forces changes in their life styles. As a person gets more closely in touch with how stagnant and dead his marriage is, he needs to decide what he will *do* about the situation. He can challenge the relationship, change it, or possibly decide to dissolve the marriage.

In the many groups in which I have participated, I am not aware of anyone being destroyed psychologically nor has anyone had a psychotic break. What I have found is that each of us has a sense of how deeply involved we want to become. When it gets "too hot," people have simply turned off by going to sleep, becoming defensive, or leaving.

A criticism is sometimes leveled at marathon encounter groups as a form of instant therapy, perhaps because some enthusiasts claim that a few of these experiences can provide a new life, expand awareness, and provide ultimate joy. I think it is fair to say that marathons can be a good beginning in this direction. However, this process should not be considered an end in itself. Individual psychotherapy as an adjunct to a series of marathons can be most helpful. The marathon itself has real value in setting the atmosphere for release of feeling, but individual therapy is often needed to help a person work through, explore, and integrate these feelings.

A question frequently raised is what happens to people when they shed their defenses and open themselves up. What if the entire group bombards them with negative feelings and hostility? In my experiences I've rarely seen this happen. There may be some groups that focus on unleashing hostility, but this depends largely on the philosophy of the leader. Feelings of anger toward others need to be expressed and worked through, but again this is not an end in itself. After the negative feelings are expressed, positive feelings (such as affection, concern, caring, warmth) need to be expressed. This demands an atmosphere of caring and trust, which is not achieved by a ruthless tearing down of each member.

Another danger often cited is that the person leaving might find himself alone and unable to deal with all that came out in the group. This is a real possibility, and for this reason I recommend individual counseling sessions at least be available to the participants so they can further explore areas of difficulty. This is another reason for having a follow-up group of all the members. If I were to say that there were no risks or dangers involved here it would be a lie. A process cannot have all this potential value for growth without also containing certain risks.

I want to emphasize one message: *the real value of the group is found to the extent that we can transfer what we learned in the group to the outside world.* A sort of reality testing can occur in the group, but if these gains are to be relatively permanent parts of us, we need to make links with the outside world. It may take time, but eventually the particpant learns that in the real world, as well as in the group, increased awareness and growth is sometimes worth the price of the necessary risk.

A METHOD OF MINIMIZING RISKS

To decide who gets admitted to a group course and to minimize the negative outcomes and dangers, I do require a personal interview with each applicant. In this conference I describe what we do in groups and why, say something of the purpose, and introduce the format used. This interview is done on an individual basis. Further, we have an initial three-hour group meeting for this purpose. I ask each person to read several articles on the nature and purposes of encounter groups. During the individual interview, I attempt to discover if the person is psychologically "ready" for such an experience and provide him with an opportunity to ask any questions to decide if he wants to be involved in this experience. I'm not trying to "play God" and create an elite society; rather I'm attempting to exercise some reasonable precautions in excluding shoppers, observers, and people who simply want to satisfy their curiosity. Also, these groups are designed for relatively well-adjusted "normals" who wish to learn ways of actualizing their potential more fully, and not for treating or curing emotionally ill persons. I have excluded people who evidence deep-seated psychological conflicts, as I felt that the intensity of such a group might be more damaging than constructive for them.

MY VIEW OF GROUP AND
MY ROLE AS A GROUP LEADER

I find that I am resistant to subscribing to any singular theoretical model of counseling—either individually or in groups. What seems important is that I synthesize a personal approach that is an outgrowth of my own personality. Perhaps I could be labeled as an "electically-oriented existential humanist." What this means is that I am attempting to integrate and synthesize a number of various approaches to encounter groups. Here is summary of my view of a group: the group is a microcosm of society. In the group situation we have a behavior sample of how we relate to others. From the feedback we receive in this situation, we obtain a picture of how we are perceived, of the messages we send out, and of the impact of our life style upon the other person in the relationship. We can decide for ourselves, through experimenting with alternative behaviors, what kinds of changes we wish to make for ourselves. We compare our self-perception with how we are perceived by others; we open ourselves to certain risks; we confront and are confronted; and most important of all, we have a confrontation with self. We use the encounter group as a place to ask ourselves questions such as: What are the various dimensions of *me?* How do I function in relationships? What potentials within me are locked up, what is keeping them sealed up, and how can I remove obstacles to maximize my potential? What do I value? How did I arrive at these values? Which values do I want to modify, retain, or reject? How do I see myself now, and how would I like to be five or ten years hence? What conflicts within me are yet unresolved, and how is this manifested in my day-to-day behavior?

These are but a few of the concerns we have in group encounters. It is useful to stay with a here-and-now orientation as much as possible and even to exclude the outside world for a time. To experience the present moment fully is worth striving for. Then we attempt to carry outside into our real living that which we learned about ourselves in the group situation. The aim is to extend ourselves in our outside world by continuing to engage in risk-taking, initiating, experimenting behavior.

One of the most significant aspects of this group process is that we get closely in touch with our own power. We often tend to be apologetic about accepting our power (strengths, talents, assets, and positive impact upon other persons). For me, the most gratifying part of a group is sharing in each person's realization that he can be powerful. This power grows out of the person's recognition of self-worth and of his potential to be the kind of person he chooses to work toward becoming.

As a group leader, I do provide structure for the group. I initiate, direct, help participants to define their own working goals; I attempt to lay a foundation conducive to love and trust so that members will feel free enough to explore unknown territory; I suggest certain techniques when they seem appropriate to what is happening at the present moment; and I assist the group to establish a degree of cohesion so they can work through barriers. Generally, I am far more active in the beginning stages of a group; I gradually expect the group members to assume many of the leadership functions. In fact, for me a partial gauge of the success of a group is the degree to which I am no longer needed as *the* group leader, so that instead we have as many leaders as we have members.

I am still struggling with my role as group leader. I'm convinced that I don't want to be an objective and detached "professional" leader. Becoming personally involved, when appropriate, seems to facilitate the process. If I find myself becoming bored or detached, impatient, intolerant, uncaring, or whatever, then I feel it necessary to share these reactions. I very much want to reveal what I am experiencing in the group as I am experiencing it—be it a positive or negative feeling. In short, I'd like to be, or at least attempt to be, what I urge and expect of the rest of the participants.

THE USE OF TECHNIQUES IN GROUPS

Basically, I have borrowed many special techniques that I have learned from other therapists and through my reading, but I do attempt to adapt these techniques to my own unique style. I am becoming more resistant to simply introducing these techniques, for I have discovered that they can boomerang. If I introduce "gimmicks" during the initial phase, the participants tend to become passive, to respond more than initiate, and to wait for the leader to turn them on or to make something happen when they experience a plateau. I prefer to introduce a technique when it feels right or when it is appropriate to what someone is feeling. This lessens the risk of it becoming a mechanical gimmick.

I am often told that encounter techniques are unreal, staged, and artificial. As an example, when a person is filled with rage as he is expressing his feelings toward his father, who never acknowledged his existence, I might ask him to express these feelings nonverbally to the pillow in front of him on the floor. He will counter that that is phony. After a few punches, however, it *does* become *very* real; and he finds a way to get close to feelings that formerly were inaccessible.

GROUP EXPERIENCE FOR EVERYBODY?

Should every teacher be involved in an encounter group? Do we all need this kind of experience? Aren't there other ways of growth? These questions are often asked. I do not favor mandatory encounter groups. I strongly support the concept of a personal choice and commitment, for the intensive and personal kind of learning that occurs in group cannot be forced upon anyone. Each person must decide for himself if he is willing to expose himself to a potentially painful (or joyful) experience that might be a most significant occurrence in his life.

One of my strong convictions is that anyone who is a "people helper" (teachers, counselors, social workers, psychologists, nurses, ministers, etc.) owes it to the people they serve to be actualizing persons. Ethically, I cannot assist a client or student to face problems if I myself have not faced or struggled with my problems. I see the encounter group as one means of becoming more of a person and as a way of increasing the chances of having a therapeutic, positive, significant effect upon those we teach or counsel. You need to decide for yourself if you want to become involved in a group for this to occur, or if you think a group is necessary. There are other avenues to growth. I also think it is a mistake to view the encounter group as an end in itself. It is *a means* to the end of helping us become more complete humans, but it should be recognized that there are a multitude of approaches to growth.

SOME INHIBITING STYLES OF
GROUP PARTICIPATION

There are some styles of behaving in a group which hinder the development of a cohesive and working group. The following are ten stereotyped roles that I find are detrimental to a group.

1. *The Encounter Group Bum.* This person has made encounter groups as a way of life. He lives for group meetings, and they have become an end in themselves. He has divorced himself from the real world and found safe harbor in encountering.

2. *The Nurse.* This is the helpful person who is constantly vigilant for any opportunity to help others. It can be a male nurse as well as a female nurse. This person often jumps in and wants to cheer up people who are experiencing pain. Instead of letting them experience their feelings fully, the helpful nurse urges the person to count his blessings and be thankful that things aren't worse than they are!

3. *The Intellectualizer.* The intellectualizing type makes constant references to books, theories, universal concepts—anything to pull the group away from intense here-and-now feelings that might be generating the group. Because he is afraid of experiencing his own feelings, he often attempts to divert the group to a head level.

4. *The Interrogator.* Then there is the cross-examiner. His style is to bombard people with questions such as: "Why do you feel that way?" "What caused that problem?" "Why don't you. . . . ?" This becomes an endless and fruitless game—a question is posed, the interrogated one answers, and any feeling is lost!

5. *The Storyteller.* Some members need to recite their entire life history from infancy to the present. They give you every detail of what happened to them, and then usually proceed to rationalize their present behavior on the basis of their past history. The message is: "How can I be blamed for what I am now, because others made me what I am?" By dwelling upon past history, the present never needs to be faced or dealt with.

6. *The Lover.* The lover is always in search for a free feel. His main interest is encountering, preferably in a nonverbal way—by hugging, touching, etc. The problem with the lover is that he is not honest with what he wants or needs. Instead he uses the group as a socially accepted way to get or give "love." I am not saying that touching, embracing, and other nonverbal forms of behaving that are often a part of encounter groups ought to be avoided. My concern is that a group ought to be more than what is sometimes called a "feely group."

7. *The Quiet Seducer.* This is the person who blends into the wood-work most of the evening, until finally other group members urge him to come out. They become ensnarled in his seductive trap. His message is, "Damned if I'll give you anything of me—if you appreciate me, then you'll draw me out!"

8. *The Thank-God-I'm-Not-Like-the-Rest-of-These-Sickies Type.* This is the person who sits back and critically observes group activity, but rarely gets involved by sharing his own feelings. When members confront him for being a voyeur, he retorts with: "I just can't understand all this time we spend on problems! Why are you all dwelling upon your misery? I don't feel any of the things all you sick ones experience. I'm okay!!"

9. *The Hostile Attacker.* There are self-appointed aggressive people who feel that cutting people down to size is of value. This type of person in a subtle and underhanded way utters caustic remarks, throws out barbs, and takes special delight in attacking other group members. If a member confronts another directly out of concern for that person, that is fine; the hostile attacker, however, shows no care, love, or cncern.

10. *If Only It Weren't For. . . .* ! In every group we discover the type of person who is sure that his life would be vastly improved if it weren't for his wife, mother, father, boss . . . This type of person avoids coming to grips with personal responsibility and puts the burden for his life situation upon another's shoulders.

RESULTS:
DIRECTIONS TAKEN BY THE PARTICIPANTS

What are the outcomes of a successful group, particularly in terms of individual changes in the participants? It is difficult to determine what constitutes a "good group." I don't put much value on factors such as how many people wept, or how many dramatic events occured, or how many people left feeling "high" and "super turned-on." A working group seems to be characterized by a willingness of the participants to disclose more than their superficial selves; trust persons in the group; open up and share what they are presently experiencing; take initiative and assume many of the leadership functions; empathize with and understand the world as it is experienced by the others; become involved, or if uninvolved, so state; and attempt consciously to transmit what they learned in group to their relationships with the people with whom they live, work, and play on the outside.

The best way to describe the outcomes of a group experience is to read actual accounts of the participants themselves. Later in this chapter (pp. 95–102) I have included portions of participants' reports so you can get a view of what group is like for those who experienced it. In general, I see participants moving in these directions:

- They learn to be more trusting of both their own feelings and the feelings of others.
- They become more willing to open up and share with another those parts of themselves they formerly concealed.
- They become less defensive and less closed, and move toward more openness to new experiencing and toward more flexible, experimental, and spontaneous ways of behaving.
- They frequently work through unresolved conflicts and dichotomies within themselves that prevent them from becoming what they choose to become.
- They tend to challenge their values and attitudes; some modification toward more internally-derived values occurs.
- They tend to work more for their own approval than the other's approval.

REENTRY INTO THE REAL WORLD

Do people experience difficulty in leaving the group and going back home? Are the gains made in the group lasting or merely temporary? It is not uncommon to hear a member say, "Why can't the outside world be like our group? Why can't we be as honest and trusting out there as we are in here?" Sometimes people attempt to be direct and confronting *outside* and find that they are neither appreciated nor rewarded for their uninvited honesty. They may ask and not receive. They may level with a friend and alienate that person. They soon find out that they need to be selective and discriminating. What *is* important to realize is that increased intimacy with selected persons is possible. If we want more intense, real, and vital relationships, they can be found with *some* people.

The question of whether the gains made in an encounter group are of a permanent or temporary nature is difficult to answer. Surely, one group experience is not enough. Self-learning and self-development is an ongoing and continual process. Reinforcement of new learning is essential. If you are exposed to a group and make some changes, some form of support and feedback seems crucial if these changes are to be integrated into your personality. I see the answer to this question depending largely upon how seriously an individual wants to remain open to change and growth and how willing he is to work for these changes.

FOLLOW-UP PROCEDURES

To determine the effectiveness of a particular group, each member is asked to write a report describing what the experience of the group was like, how the group affected him, how he is using what he learned in group on the outside, what the high points and low points of the group were, what unfinished business he has with personal conflicts or with people in the group, and so on. In essence, the report serves the purpose of helping crystalize the value of the group for each person, as well as giving the leader increased insight to the dynamics of that group.

Further, we schedule several three-hour follow-up group meetings to share our post-reactions. Often I will write to members one year later to get some idea of the lasting value and effectiveness of a particular group upon each individual. In general, the results of these groups are positive; and I have seen persons drastically alter their lives in directions they see as satisfying and deeply meaningful. The group can be a catalyst for either subtle or dramatic modifications of life style. Following is a letter I recently received from a woman who had been in two of these groups describing some ways the groups have influenced her life one year after the experiences.

FOLLOW-UP EVALUATION: A LETTER FROM A PARTICIPANT ONE YEAR LATER

At long last I am replying to your request for follow-up information on the encounter group experiences I had last year. Although I wrote our detailed answers last fall and verbally expressed some of my ideas to you, I am now ready to submit my evaluation.

Without sounding overly dramatic, I must say that the group experiences were a turning point in my life. Perhaps the time was right and the need was tremendous, but I feel like a very different person today from the timid soul who talked her way into the fall group in September. The results have been lasting, the basis for continued growth, increasing awareness of and sensitivity to my world.

Pursuant to your questions, I must say that the group experience gave me the opportunity to face myself for the first time—to look back at my life up to that point with an attempt to see myself honestly, lucidly, nakedly, as it were, without hiding behind barriers of false pride or modesty or the mask of a role player. Coupled with my own insight gained from introspection was the response I gained from others who knew me, as only Mary, a person, a fellow human being. It was refreshing to interact with other persons purely as human beings, to sense and share their worries, fears, joys, love—a great range of emotions. Probably one of the greatest benefits of participating in a group is realizing that everyone has "hang-ups," and has made ridiculous (sometimes even tragic) mistakes, has limitations yet has such a tremendous capacity for life. The realization that one does not have to be the victim of past mistakes, that today is the first day of the rest of your life, so to speak, that each person must choose for himself to live (or not to live)—to say, "damn it, I'm responsible for *me!*" is one of the greatest gifts the group can give. I am not naively suggesting that the group bestows this gifts. You know that I know a person must work like hell to derive real results.

While participating in the groups I felt as if I was deeply involved, risking much, trusting, giving, seeking. I experienced the "highs" you mentioned (which I discussed at length in immediate follow-up papers) and have experienced greater "lows" but this is good for me, I believe, because I have greatly expended the range of emotions I feel. I now allow myself to feel "negative" feelings and to express them openly, even emphatically or savagely. How about that!

Enduring gains seem to be these at this point:

1. A greater confidence in myself as a person with unique qualities, with a sense of controlling my own life to a much greater extent.
2. An expanded awareness of other persons and a much greater openness and willingness to trust, risk and love.
3. Much increased ability to listen to my children—to hear beyond the words to deeper meanings—to share thoughts, feelings, concerns with them.
4. Most important, my relationship with my husband has very definitely been altered. After surviving the confrontations following the groups which seemed to threaten him so much, we have achieved unbelieveable dimensions together. Of course, we still have confrontations, but they are healthy ones now with each of us aware of the need to resolve differences. I no longer snap up the bait that used to start unreasonable, ridiculous disagreements. My husband seldom tries to manipulate my feelings now as he seems to see me in an altogether different way.
5. The awareness that at times we must become so confused that it is necessary to seek help. I am sure that my sons will seek help if they ever need it because they have seen what a difference it can make in life. They are so relieved to know that Henry is getting things sorted out in his own mind. Knowing that it is possible to reach out to someone for help is quite a thing—like a giant step

forward in being able to live life freely and fully. I might add that although it took Henry over a year to finally seek help, he has realized and acknowledged the wisdom of getting help and has even urged other people to do so. To reach that point himself was more difficult. But he made it, thank goodness.

The bad effects, as far as I am concerned, were related to my husband's distrust of the experience and his ridicule of the group. His fear of my participating could have had tragic results, but, fortunately, we survived and now have gone so far beyond that unsettled time that I see nothing lasting but strong, positive results.

I would recommend an encounter group experience (and have) to my friends, although I would urge anyone who contemplates participating in a group to read *Joy* (89) or *Let Me Live* (65) or *On Becoming a Person* (75) or some of the newer books (at least one description of a group) to have some awareness of what to expect. I think the eight-hour sessions were better for a first experience, although maybe I say that because it worked well for me. The intensity of a long marathon might really frighten a beginner, especially if he attends a session like the two we had in spring. All things considered, I would recommend a group experience to anyone who wants to become more alive, more aware, more sensitive to himself and others.

Once again, thank you for your leadership, your belief in the underlying goodness of people, your trust, inspiration and wisdom.

ENCOUNTER—AS PARTICIPANTS EXPERIENCE IT

For the reader who wishes to learn more about the process and outcomes of encounter groups, I suggest any of several recent books. Schutz's book *Joy* (89) describes first-person accounts of marathon group experiences. Carl Roger's recent book, *Carl Rogers on Encounter Groups* (88), is useful and easy to read on the process and outcomes of encounter groups. Egan's *Encounter: Group Process for Interpersonal Growth* (81) is an excellent summary of the research on various types of sensitivity groups. Lyon's *Let Me Live* (65) is another highly recommended book.

My intent is not to write another book on encounter groups; rather I hope to give you some flavor of what occurs in these groups, what process develops, and what outcomes occur for the participants. In the following pages you will be reading first-person accounts from the participants themselves. To disguise identities, I have taken reports from several groups during the past year, and selected statements which in my judgment reflect genuine feeling experiences within the participants of these teacher groups.

I WANT TO GROW, BUT I'M FRIGHTENED

As I look back tonight upon the first Saturday, I see myself very frightened—terribly anxious. I tried to think of so many excuses that I might avoid going, but something made me go. I wanted to grow . . .

GETTING IN TOUCH WITH THE SOURCE OF LONELINESS

I'm working on becoming a more giving person—not just to others, but to me. I've been so lonely all this time because I deserted myself. I need me and I'd never have admitted that three weeks ago. How can I give to others when I can't give to myself? For the first time I feel I can give to myself, and it's a good feeling. I'm looking forward to the future, not with dread, but with excited enthusiasm.

I WANT APPROVAL AND ACCEPTANCE

I want a great deal of approval and acceptance, but not a great deal of closeness. I can hardly stand to be rejected by anyone. Maybe that is why I have gone along with my parents so long.

NEW LEVELS OF SENSORY AWARENESS

Another thing I want to make note of is a change in my awareness of sensations. For example, I just came in from having a swim. The water felt so much more beautiful than ever before. I just realized and floated and floated and let it envelop me. What a luxurious experience! My sense of taste, too, has become so much more acute. I don't seem to need much food to be satisfied, as I usually do. I just had an apricot (I got two out of the refrigerator, but only needed to eat one). As I was eating it, I really allowed myself to totally experience the taste and feel of it in my mouth. The sensation was almost overpowering. I guess I'm starting to become that horrible hedonist—but it's a good feeling. It scares me to think of all the things in life I've just semi-appreciated, taking all the little things for granted.

GROUP EXPERIENCES DO RELATE TO THE REAL WORLD

I keep thinking about our group and how that experiences can be utilized in the real world. One thing for sure . . . it was not a contrived experience. Everything we said or did can occur on the outside if one is willing to take the risk. If one wants to have something deeper with those that are important to you, then the encounter experience can be of great significance to helping you find those feelings that enable you to open up to others. I like our honesty and genuineness.

A CELEBRATION OF SELF:
APPRECIATING AND ACCEPTING ONE'S OWN WORTH AS A PERSON

I found myself far less interested in other people's problems in these sessions—far more appreciative of the good things people wanted to give to me—enjoyed the good things people gave me—and really realized the richness and attractiveness of me—the aging, lonely, unloved, abandoned me became far more desireable. I became a really attractive commodity—and I became aware (perhaps for the first time) of the uniqueness of me—that out of those years of slow and sometimes painful evolution of myself emerged someone that had special gifts and powers—that I could afford not to give—not to please—I could stand still long enough to receive—and the staying power of my personality was strong enough and the positive identity of me was rich enough to hold the interest and affection of people. I did not have to bear gifts constantly—*I* was a gift—*I* was a source of joy—not by saving or rescuing others—but just by projecting me. As I write this I am celebrating me—and it feels damn good. I really deserve everything people are giving me—I don't want "rabbit turds" or the love of weak, helpless, immature women—I want some of the good stuff—now! not as a special reward for some good deed or because it's a holiday—but because I deserve it. I am going to buy some T-shirts (the ones I have are full of holes and are grey), my wallet is falling apart and needs to be replaced, my closet is almost empty and I am going to buy some clothes, I am going to get a file cabinet for my papers—I am going to get that damn doctorate, etc., etc., etc.

DIVORCE FROM MY MOTHER: BEGINNING TO LIVE BY INTERNAL VALUES

It is completely impossible to describe what and how this week-end took place. All I can say is, eighteen people became very honest and open with each other to the point many probably never would have shared if it had not been for trust, love, and honesty. As probably you have already guessed, something very significant happened to me. I broke down emotionally, mentally and physically and gave out my feelings at the gut level. It was my mother. As I know you probably already know, I am sick up to my head of trying to please her—trying to be accepted by her—trying to meet her standards and rules. I love her but I *cannot* and *will not* adhere to her whims again!!! I have my own life to lead, and there are things I want to do and a lot of them don't agree with hers but I'm living my own life!! I already discovered how I don't even know my true feelings anymore. For so many years I've been trying to please and think like Mother that the me is lost. I can't be true to myself because I don't know myself. But I'll be damned if I'll be pushed around again. I'm tired of being stepped on, and only used to please someone else. I do realize I'm in the state of rebellion, but it has to come if my own independence is going to be a living vital reality. I need to confront others, but I fear it will make me hard as I have seen it already do. I can no longer be sweet and submissive to the degree that others walk over me. I'm so sick of it—gosh, I'm sick of the entire mess—always trying to please —trying to squeeze into someone's mold. You don't know how good it makes me feel to make this decision. I'm afraid it may have never come if it hadn't been for this week-end.

A PERSONAL DECLARATION OF INDEPENDENCE

As the process went on I was aware that something was happening inside. It was like a key was put in a lock and chains were being lifted off my arms, legs and heart. For the first time I was free—really free—it felt so good—there was so much I felt like doing—wanting to run and tell the wide world that this was my day—my independence day—and the me was born. As the Declaration of Independence set many ideals for the new United States, I knew the Constitution for my own life would take some time to write and put into practive. I'm beginning to feel a little of the frustration and anxiety Jefferson and Franklin must have felt.

TEACHERS ARE PEOPLE, TOO!

Although I feel I have always been fairly open and personally accessible as a teacher to my students, I find that I am risking more with them. In music and literature I did a talking, singing, playing guitar presentation of ballads in front of a huge number of kids many of whom are tremendously more accomplished at playing and singing than I. I was scared shitless! But I found it to be a humanizing experience. They were very appreciative, and even enjoyed it. More significantly, they learned that teachers are people, too.

STRANGERS BECAME MEANINGFUL PEOPLE

Group experience was for me frightening and exhilarating all at once. It was the most rewarding experience I have ever had in relating, communicating, and interacting with human beings. The group situation in itself is not realistic in that it is too ideal—you exist within the group only for twenty hours. What I learned about myself was very real, and what I am doing about what I learned in my outside life is also very real and rewarding. My biggest fear in the group experience was that I would not be able to risk and therefore would not be able to gain. I was afraid of defeat, afraid that I would cop out. I didn't. I became so emotionally intimate with twenty people, I grew to trust them and for the first time I experienced sincere confidence in dealing with and relating to adults. I learned a lot about myself and a lot about other people. I really recognized the importance of honesty, interaction, and communication. I feel that I have really grown and broadened myself from the experience.

WE CAN LEARN TO RISK IF WE TRUST

I'm home, I'm ecstatic, I can't sleep . . . , right now I feel as beautiful as life itself feels to me at this moment. Tomorrow it may seem like shit as it sometimes does, but that can't rob me of this night's profound experiences. God, I'm thankful! I didn't cop out, I got involved, I gave and the group gave back and damn it, I want more. I'm more aware of being "hungry" now than I've ever been before. At this point I still don't know who in the hell I am or what I really want from life, but damn it, I want to risk enough to find out. I feel as though yesterday I brought myself in a little box, scared shitless to climb out, but I did climb out and better yet, I think I threw that damn box away. A horrifying fright and basic distrust of twenty strangers in twenty hours was converted to feelings like trust (for the group as a whole), caring, touching, loving, giving and taking for many individuals. Damn, it felt good, and out came honesty—no games. It was real and we lived it. For the first time in my life I loved twenty brand new people all at one time recognizing that this love didn't strip me of the right to hate them also and tell them off if I felt like it.

I FEEL OPEN

In retrospect, I must say I have never been so totally open before, anywhere. I felt and did things I believed myself incapable of doing, or things I never considered. I felt a warm glow, a love for the group. I was full of love, for the very first time in my life.

As I write this I am crying like a baby. Not because I am overwhelmingly sad or happy (although I am happy), but because I haven't slept for the past three nights, since our meeting on Saturday. Since our last two meetings I have been unable to sleep, I keep thinking and evaluating myself and the group. I try to survey what I received and if I gave as much as I could have. Now my eyes are so red. They really are burning. It hurts to open them and to close them, and I am all out of eyedrops. It was an experience worth a dozen burning eyes.

THEY BECAME SPECIAL PEOPLE TO ME

Saturday I went home with hope. It seemed that time dragged until our next meeting. I wanted it to come faster. I admired Karen's openness Sunday morning, and realized as she spoke that each member of the group had taken on a special meaning. They were not just any people, but special people whom I loved, though I knew none of the usual facts about them.

I'M LEARNING TO FEEL MORE FEMININE

Sunday was definitely the most wonderful day of all. I actually could *feel* the intensity and the closeness of the group. I felt safer than I have ever felt before. I've always hated the way I saw myself (sort of prim and dowdy and colorless) but I never knew that I could do anything about my self-concept. It's really neat how feminine I feel if I just think I am—I hope it shows. Like most girls I suppose, I've been brought up to suppress my sexual feelings and as a result, to deny my sexuality. I've never given myself a chance to be moral, I've never thought I could be sexually appealing, I've never admitted to myself that I had any sexual feelings about men. I feel like a fool now saying this at 24, but it's true. My idea of morality was denial of sexuality. I'm beginning to realize that I'm denying a very important part of me by not admitting to myself that I am a woman. I'm sure I'm not going to overcome this hang-up easily though."

INITIAL REACTIONS AND IMPRESSIONS

When we arrived for the first session, I sensed an air of expectation and uncertainty. It seemed as if we talked for a long time about the nature of the course, requirements, etc., yet I was getting anxious to begin work. I was impressed with the setting, with the relaxed, subdued atmosphere in the room. People seemed friendly yet a bit apprehensive. As we began trying to focus on ourselves, imagining our greatest fear within the group, I was uncertain. Gradually a fantasy came into my mind picturing me just sitting there while all kinds of activity was going on around me. I really felt fear with cold hands, sweaty palms, dry throat, gnawing stomach. When you put your hands on my shoulders indicating my turn to speak my fear, I sensed strength and acceptance of me—of each of us—as a real, genuine member of the group. I really wanted to participate. I felt compassion for people who were afraid to expose themselves to the group. I guess I realized that I had been through that and at this point in my life was more afraid of deceiving myself, realizing that although I may expose myself to the world as a fraud, I must obtain a clearer understanding of who I am, of what I am worth as a person, as a human being without regard for what I have done or what I can do or who I am as a member of society.

BEFORE AND AFTER REACTIONS TO ENCOUNTER GROUPS

To be perfectly honest, when I came to the first group meeting I thought encounter groups were dumb, probably because of my ignorance of my own feelings. I resented the fact that you called it a therapy group because I wasn't sick and I certainly didn't need psychiatric help (I thought). I wondered aloud on the way to the meeting if people didn't have to be kind of freaky to react to other people. Today I'm almost ashamed that I really could not see how people could ever elicit a response from me. I think it would be appropriate to make a brief comment on my feelings about encounter groups—having now had this wonderful experience. I can't explain my feelings with words, it's just impossible, and this really pleases me. For once in my life I'm able to alienate what I think from what I feel, and its nice not to be able to put those feelings into words. The curiosity that brought me to the class surely paid off—I got so much more than I bargained for.

I CAN EXPRESS EMOTION

I have learned that I *can* express emotion to other people, other men and women. I can give and I can *take* selfishly, to thirst and hunger and ravenously seek satisfaction and satisfaction and satiation. I know that my richest source of fullness and completeness, of ecstasy, is with my husband for our love continues to grow in spite of (or perhaps because of) problems.

LEARNING TO ACCEPT PERSONAL RESPONSIBILITY

As the first day progressed, I thought a lot about my father. I've always considered him strong and decisive, but never before did I realize that I was letting him stifle me. For two weeks I kept asking myself the question you asked me—"How old are you anyway?" I've come to the conclusion that I can no longer blame what I am on my dad. If I'm dependent and blah, I can only blame me. Saturday I left having resolved to think for myself and please myself first. After all, who is more important to please? You might be interested to know, though, that one cannot have her own feelings or opinions or ideas and live in my father's house. I've been told when and where to do everything for so long that when I question myself honestly, I have trouble deciding if something is what *I* really want or just a comfortable habit. I have to get away and be me—I want to live my own life for *me* for awhile and I've started doing just that.

EMPATHY AND CONCERN

When Betsy revealed her burden of sorrow, I wanted to help her, to tell her that such a mistake is human, that she must not punish herself endlessly for making it. I wanted her to release the poison of her guilt which could destroy her chances of happiness. When we "buried" her, I "died" with her for I realized that a living death could be more horrible than actual death because you continue to suffer and realize it day after day. It really was dramatic to think of all of us around her coffin, covering her with dirt, then condemning her to a life of loneliness and despair. How strongly I wanted her to demand life. When she said, "I want to live!" I cheered for her and shouted it with her (inside) for I know that I too wanted to live.

I DECIDED TO LIVE AGAIN

The most beautiful part was the reactions I got as I went around the room. These people told me things I shall never forget as long as I live. I get tears in my eyes when I think about them. When I get doubts, I think of those beautiful words and it really gives me courage. I know I am by no means "cured," but it made me decide that I do want to live again. I want to become a real live human being again. I'm not going to shuffle around with my head down anymore. The people in that room made me want to grab onto myself again.

SHARING IN JOY AND ECSTASY

The group was marvelous to me, letting me thrash about with my feelings, listening, reflecting, encouraging, accepting, loving. Seeing nearly everyone risk and gain, risk more and achieve more was a rewarding experience. The changes that took place in each person— some much greater than others—were really noticeable. Laura's whole appearance changed and softened after we worked with her. Mary was a new person, a wonderful woman, after all three sessions. She did as much as anyone—more, probably, to help everyone. Even Karen cracked a little. Your work is very demanding, exhausting, yet I can understand why you are so enthusiastic and extremely effective as you guide a group of strangers through the darkness to a glowing world of love and acceptance.

The final milling around period was a fascinating summation of our experience because we had risked, shared, struggled, suffered, accepted and rejoiced together. We revealed this to each other as we gravitated toward the center of the group. I didn't want to move because the warmth and openness and love we shared was so evident. At times it seemed as if we were all together in one tightly woven ball. Joy! Ecstasy! Life!

Words can never express the depth of gratitude I feel for my experience in the group. I know that I took tremendous risks—some may have thought me a complete fool—but I don't give a damn because I gained far more than I dreamed I would. I feel strong, very much a woman in my own right and more at peace than I have ever been. I now believe I've begun and I'm going to live.

SUMMARY: KEY IDEAS IN FOCUS

From what the participants who have experienced marathon encounter groups say, there are certain trends that seem to occur for the members. Some of these directions that people in these groups move toward are:

- There is a movement toward greater willingness to accept both positive and negative feelings in self.
- The willingness to engage in risk-taking behavior, and in a new behavior, is increased.
- False fronts and stereotyped roles tend to decrease; there is a movement toward more realness as a person.
- People tend to value themselves more, and they learn to enjoy both their assets and liabilities as individuals.
- An attitude of accepting the uniqueness of each person and "allowing" that person to simply "be" develops.
- Rigid patterns of behaving are lessened, and more flexible and spontaneous behavior occurs.
- Persons make decisions on crucial life matters more than from an internal frame of reference than an external framework.
- There is an increased feeling of aliveness on all levels—sensory, physical, emotionl, interpersonal.
- The individual tends to *demand* more out of life, both for himself and for those he loves.

CONCLUDING COMMENTS

This chapter deals with the use of the encounter group as a vehicle for the personal growth of teachers. The central purpose of the group is to assist relatively healthy people to become increasingly aware of their potential as persons and to enrichen their interpersonal relationships.

I have attempted to give you a general idea of my role as a group leader, and to mention some elements I view as crucial in group work. To begin, the individuals are nervous and anticipatorily waiting for something spectacular to happen to them. As they get in touch with their own expectations and fears, the wisdom of the group becomes apparent. People do tend to move in creative ways when there is a climate of trust and care. As the level of trust rises, so does risk-taking behavior. When persons engage in personal risking, growth and new forms of behavior begin to emerge. Members confront each other, they reach out and ask for what they want, they express positive and negative feelings, and they generally become free to *be* themselves. There is less concern of what people will think and more willingness to search for what is real inside.

The group is valuable only to the extent that its members are able to translate their learnings *in* group to their transactions with people *outside* of group. Rather than being an end in itself, the group experience enables people to clarify the quality of their relationships with their families, coworkers, and friends.

6

A Humanistic Approach to
Teacher Education

I have described my efforts in working with teachers on developing their own personal beings, principally through classes which are designed with an encounter-group format. These classes, or encounter group experiences, are elective courses offered through an extension program as a part of an inservice experience for elementary and secondary teachers. In this chapter I shall explain how we attempted to facilitate learning and change in a basic undergraduate course (which is required by the state of California of all teacher candidates) known as *Psychological Foundations of Education.* This course was taught by Dr. Rodman Garrity and me for the Teacher Preparation Center at California State Polytechnic University at Pomona during the last five years. Since this course is not an elective, special problems arise which I should like to discuss. I hope to give you a clear view of the nature of this course, my approach and philosophy, some methods of achieving important goals, and some outcomes of this course. Similar courses are a part of most, if not all, teacher education programs.

THE TRADITIONAL APPROACH

In California applicants for an elementary and secondary teaching credential are required to complete a course in educational psychology or psychological foundations of education. In most schools of education, a traditional approach is used. The professor gives lectures on such standard topics as child and adolescent development, motivation, learning theory, learning, basics of research design including statistics, animal studies and experiments, mental hygiene of the learner, group process, fundamentals of measurement and evaluation techniques, guidance procedures, and conditions for effective teaching–learning. Students generally are armed with notebook, pen, and a standard textbook in education psychology which covers (sometimes in encyclopedic form) these topics. These students are almost always required to take midterm and final examinations, along with some occasional quizzes. Because of the large number of students in these classes, most of these evaluation measures rely on "objective" approaches," i.e., true–false, multiple choice, and matching exercises.

MY FEELINGS ABOUT THIS TRADITIONAL APPROACH

It seems paradoxical that those who "teach" people how to be teachers often employ the dullest, most sterile, unimaginative, and archaic methods in their classes, while expecting these same students to kindle wild enthusiasm in their own creative classrooms! How are they to learn ways of exciting students to learning? From that example? Or from carefully observing their teachers present themselves and their courses and then doing the opposite?

In a conventional course in educational psychology the students show up, take notes, listen dutifully to lectures, write term papers, summarize journal articles, and find ways of "passing" the examinations. The trouble with this approach is simply that they pass through the course forgetting much of what they supposedly "learned" as soon as they leave the final examination. Often they forget the entire experience by the time they are doing student teaching. What they learned was external; since the course content had little *personal* meaning, very little was integrated and applied to later experience in student teaching.

I feel that we who work in teacher education ought to be in the forefront with educational innovation and experimentation. We are the ones who should take the risk of abandoning traditional methods which are used largely because of security, comfort, and ease. Our courses ought to deal with issues that have relevant meaning, and we should seek to stimulate the interest of our students in the same way we expect them to do with their future students. My bias is toward the definite directions of the *humanistic, existential,* and *person-centered* approaches to education.

THE COURSE CONTENT

What are some of the issues dealt with in Psychological Foundations of Education? What is the nature of this course? Many of the conventional topics in educational psychology are treated in my course, but not in the conventional way. The course is drawn from such facets of psychology as child development, adolescent psychology, and social psychology. Some of the issues, problems, topics, questions, and avenues of exploration might include the following:

1. What are some of the experiences of childhood that we lose as we become adults?
2. What are the various stages of development of children, and what psychological–social needs are most crucial at each stage?
3. What is the optimal psychological climate that fosters growth, wholeness, and health in children and adolescents?
4. What forces have an impact upon the contemporary adolescent? What problems are unique to this stage of development? Can the school meet the personal needs of adolescents?
5. How much freedom can children and youth constructively cope with? Can they learn freedom with responsibility, and can they initiate their own learning?
6. Why the drop-out problem? What can be done to prevent school drop-outs? What do students say about their education and about their teachers?
7. What are the destructive effects of traditional education upon the learner? What does formal schooling do to us? Is *education* really possible in school? What are the forces militating against free and creative learning?
8. Are changes within the existing school system feasible? Can substantial change be made? What are the barriers to change? What changes are most needed?
9. How do children learn? And how do they fail? What kind of learning atmosphere is necessary for authentic learning to occur?
10. What is the meaning of education? What is the purpose of education? Is there a difference between training and education?
11 What are some viable alternatives to conventional education? What alternatives are possible now? What are some forms of experimentation currently in operation in education?
12. Is humanistic, person-centered, psychological education possible with our current school system? How does humanistic education differ from other forms of education?
13. Why is the personal growth of the teacher such a vital component in the teaching-learning process?
14. Is the model of authenticity of teacher's being necessary for real learning to occur?
15. What are some dimensions of the teacher as a person? What are ways teachers can work on their personal growth and self-awareness? Can the teacher be an instrument in facilitating constructive change within the classroom?
16. Why do people become teachers anyway? What are some of the psychological dynamics of selecting teaching as a career?
17. What does our own schooling do to us as learners? And what effects will this have upon us as teachers? Will we teach in the same way as we were taught?

18. Can we really make a significant difference in the lives of the
    students we teach? What is the range and scope of our power as
    teachers? Do we recognize our power, and how do we use or
    abuse it?
19. What is informal education? Can we free ourselves of our past
    conditioning and provide our students with genuine freedom to
    learn? How can we help students to become more self-directed
    learners?
20. What are some ways of evaluating and assessing the outcomes of
    learning? Why is the process of self-evaluation essential?

THE PURPOSE OF THE COURSE

My goal is not to provide an objective survey course covering all
of the standard topics in educational psychology. As can be seen in
a review of this list of questions reflecting the course content, the
experience is more of a philosophy of educational psychology than a
course that deals with research findings related to learning.

The central purpose of my course is to encourage future teachers
to reflect upon their own experiences as a learner and to become aware
of the implications these learnings have for them *as teachers.* A major
goal is to encourage each student to come to grips with significant
questions (related to the psychology of education) and to explore these
issues through extensive reading and discussion seminars.

Another central aim is to assist students in selecting books that can
be useful in exploring issues which have aroused their interest. If the
desire to read, and to think critically about this reading, takes root in
this course, it will most likely continue after the course is formally
completed.

MY PHILOSOPHY APPLIED TO THE COURSE

I believe each person must each find for himself a style that is
compatible with his own philosophy and what he is as a person. To
mimic another's style because it works well for him is a sure invitation
to failure. I experiment with each class I teach, but I do not consider
my students the objects of this experimentation. I experiment myself
with new ideas, with approaches that I would like to try, with content
variations, and with various styles and combinations of teaching.
When I began teaching at the high school level over ten years ago, I
was quite authoritarian, teacher-centered, very subject-matter con-

scious, and rather traditional! As much as I hate to admit it, aspects of this old me are still a part of my being now as a college professor in the Teacher Preparation Center. As clearly as I can tell you, here is where I am presently:

I do believe in freedom *within a structure.* I'm not the type of person that chooses to enter a classroom and ask, "Well, what do you want to do? This is *your* course, so *you* decide *what* you want to learn, and *how* you want to learn it." I am much more structured than this, yet I definitely feel that the degree of freedom I attempt to provide does allow students to pursue their own interests (at least as they broadly relate to the psychology of education).

I have certain expectations of my students; I am rather demanding of them (as I am of myself); and I have some specific requirements. Even though I have expectations and requirements, the structure is loose enough to permit individual projects and allow students to initiate and direct their own learning to as large a degree as they choose to assume.

In brief, some of my general requirements are that each student develops a reading program based upon an extensive book list dealing with a variety of themes; that each writes several thoughtful and honest reaction papers during the course on what he is learning through books, field work in the schools, class lectures, seminar groups, discussions, etc.; that each is involved in some type of field work in an elementary or secondary school working directly with learners as well as observing the dynamics of the learning process; that each student demonstrates active commitment to the course through participation in his own learning.

My philosophy is based upon the assumption that upper division and graduate level students who have elected to become teachers have the capacity to exceed even their own standards and expectations when they are provided with content that is related to their interests and personal life space. If the program is relevant and substantial, motivation is built into the course; and many of the devices used to "stimulate motivation" become unnecessary and impede learning.

Consistent with the assumption that I am dealing with mature persons who have the capacity to become self-motivated (even though this capacity may be latent), my classes have some of the following characteristics:

1. No quizzes, tests, or formal examinations are a part of the class.
2. Conventional papers are not expected. There are no research reports, summaries of journal articles, term papers, etc.

3. Reaction papers which are of a personal and subjective nature are used as more meaningful substitutes for examinations and motivational formal papers.

4. There are no assigned textbooks. Instead, students are expected to select their own reading program from interesting paperback books.

5. Each student is actively involved in some type of work with children or adolescents in a school setting, which helps make the content of the course *real.*

6. I rarely lecture *at* my students. When I do give lectures, it is usually to share my own ideas, feelings, or experiences on the topic of discussion.

7. I invite guest speakers to come to the class for sometimes as much as one-third of our class time. These guests include psychologists, principals of special schools, teachers who are involved in innovative approaches, students in high school, drop-out students, and gifted students.

8. Approximately one-third of class time is spent in seminar discussions with the professor as seminar leader–facilitator. At these seminars we share our feelings and thoughts on books being read, some issues presented for exploration, the guest speakers, and experiences related to field work in the schools.

9. Personal conferences are encouraged. I invite my students to come in to discuss anything that they care to that is raised in the course. Time is available to discuss books, reading program, problems in the field work, personal problems that become evident through readings and experience in the field, and whatever else the student wishes to discuss.

10. A few current films are shown as they seem fitting.

11. Students are encouraged to take observational field trips to special schools where innovation is occuring and where student-centered education is practiced.

12. Students are involved in the process of self-evaluation, and also in the evaluation of the course and my teaching.

THE READING PROGRAM

I have selected approximately 100 books that I highly recommend as very fitting with the humanistic slant of the course. The college bookstore orders a large quantities of each of these 100 titles, so students can purchase a series of paperback books at a price that is lower than a single textbook. My criteria for selecting these books are: (1) Are the books interesting and easy to read? (2) Will they arouse curiosity to read further? (3) Can the book generate feeling in the learner as well as generate thought? (4) Is it timely, and does it relate to the central issues in educational psychology? (5) Do students react favorably and recommend its inclusion on the list?

These books are all described in an annotated reading list that each student receives and which can be found in the appendix of this book. This way a student can select from the list the books that seem most meaningful to him. Since I expect that one book be read each week, the cost of this program can be a problem. I have arranged for the library to place a copy of each book on a limited loan basis. Also, students are encouraged to trade books with each other. I instruct my students to read these books for their *own* use. Many of them can be read like fiction. Others need to be read by making marginal notes and reflecting on key ideas. I do not test the students on the reading, but instead ask each student to discuss the *personal* meaning the book held for him. I ask that summaries be avoided. I would like to know the reactions, feelings, and thoughts students had as they read. I want to know what kinds of attitudes are being changed, what values are being challenged, what ideas are being confirmed, validated, and rejected. In essence, I want the student to share with me how he read the book, what the book means to him now, and what he feels he learned from it, if anything.

AN ALTERNATIVE TO TESTS AND EXAMINATIONS

Rarely have I felt that formal examinations measure anything of significance to the learner. *Most* of the tests teachers administer are part of the battery of techniques used to coerce students to study. I admit I'm lousy at "making" people learn, and I have found no way to interest any student who simply doesn't want to commit himself to meaningful projects. I suspect most teachers really give tests to justify grades. If a student protests that the teacher is unfair, the teacher can always justify his position by adding up the total points earned on all quizzes and tests, dividing by the number of items, and giving a formula to "prove" his "objectivity" and "fairness."

At one time I was the type of teacher who considered grades sacred, and I had a detailed formula for producing "objective" grades. Now I make no claim of being fair or objective. In fact, my system is extremely subjective. As an alternative to examinations, I ask for reaction papers about every three weeks. I expect quality in these papers in that they should give evidence that the student has been actively engaged in thinking, listening, observing, participating, reading, and reacting. These papers disclose the nature of any significant learning that seems to be emerging within the student; and if no learning is occurring, I ask them to state this honestly and attempt to understand the cause of the inertia. I'll frequently invite a student in for a conference if he feels that he is "not getting anything" from the experience. It could be due to a conflict he has with me; it could be the result of his inexperience in coping with freedom; it may be resistance to some of the challenges that are hurled at him; it may be the result of any number of factors. These papers help me keep in touch with my students, what they are learning, their negative reactions and resistances, their suggestions for reform or modifications of the program. I think this approach is far more meaningful than the usual testing method. Generally, I hate to read term papers or other impersonal papers, but I find myself carefully reading (and commenting upon) each paper—and with some enthusiasm! Believe it or not, even students find these papers a refreshing departure and welcome the opportunity to express some of their perceptions and impressions on paper.

A COMMENT ON GRADES

Grading is a problem that I admit I haven't solved yet. I've tried many approaches: given students blanket *B* grades if they merely met the requirements, asked them to suggest their own grades with justification, worked out a final grade in conference with each student, and simply subjectively decided upon the grade I felt was most appropriate. Grading is painful for both my students and myself, but it is a reality that they as teachers will someday have to face with their own students.

I would favor a Credit–No Credit approach first and a Pass–Fail basis second. Most of my students would welcome a Credit–No Credit system; but unfortunately our college still operates on the *A* through *F* system. There are some students so accustomed to grades that they *prefer* the security of *A, B, C.* This stystem, they say, lets them know exactly where they stand and what they have achieved in the professor's view. It's such a shame that anyone prefers these external symbols of his worth as a learner!

The reaction papers that I described are not graded. Instead, I make comments on each paper; if I feel a student is shirking his responsibility in the course, I tell him so on the paper and encourage him to come in to discuss the matter in a conference.

If a student wants to know "where he stands" or my evaluation of his investment in the course, he knows that he is welcome to come in for a conference to discuss this or other issues. I find that this procedure really lessens student anxiety, that it makes evaluation more of a joint effort, and that it encourages the student to assess the quality of his own investment.

FIELD WORK IN THE SCHOOLS

A complaint that most teachers have is that their teacher preparation courses seemed unreal to them. In the security of their passive roles as college students, they learn *about* children, *about* ideal conditions for learning, *about* methods of presenting subjects, and *about* motivating students. It used to be not uncommon for a teacher candidate never to set foot inside an elementary or secondary classroom from the time he left his own as a student to the time he did student teaching. When faced with the reality of being a teacher, with his own class of forty students eagerly expecting him to be himself, he gasps: "Why didn't they prepare me for this? All that stuff I learned in my education classes isn't so! What a difference between the real thing and what we were told in our education classes!"

To lessen the danger of this, and to give more assurance that the course will relate to the issues they study about, each student in my course is expected to work with children or adolescents in a school setting for a minimum of two hours weekly. Actually, most students put in double (or even triple) the minimum time. Once they really invest part of themselves in working in the field, students often find themselves robbing time from other courses to devote to field work. They find an opportunity to relate with learners in an unusual capacity: they are not simply students, but they are not really teachers with authority images either.

Each student can choose the grade level with which he wants to work, and he can select a school of his choice from over thirty schools. Rather than merely observing learners, he is encouraged to become involved with them actively in any way he chooses or any way the classroom teacher might suggest. A danger inherent in this system is that the teacher intern may be used as a clerk or to perform mechanical duties the teacher dislikes. This is another reason I ask my students to write in some detail not only what they are doing in field work, but what value they see in the experience. If problems arise, we can often make changes in the assignment.

The purpose of the field work in the schools is to give teacher candidates a first-hand opportunity to be a functioning part of the classroom, to actually experiment with teaching lessons or conducting small groups, to gain experience in tutoring, to observe the dynamics of individual and group behavior, to see the relationship between theory and practice, to gain some beginning insights into the teaching –learning process, to observe various teachers' styles of behavior and their impact upon students. The active involvement during the entire course in a public school classroom serves as a laboratory for our class. This laboratory experience allows students to test out the ideas they get from the reading program. It allows for experimentation, for challenging the concepts presented; and most of all, it is a vital aspect of helping the individual decide what kind of teacher he wants to be. It is useful in forming a personal philosophy toward learners and the learning process. And not infrequently, this experience confirms a person's desire to become a teacher *or* helps him decide that the life of a teacher is not for him, at least at that time.

MY STYLE OF BEING

I am convinced that the personality of the teacher is far a more relevant variable than his method, the content, or his procedures. So let me share with you how I see myself in the classroom, both as a person and as the person who happens to be the teacher.

To begin with, I am enthusiastic about my work. I enjoy working with students on this level; I feel inspired a good bit of the time; and I usually feel alive in my work. I think this enthusiasm spreads to my students also, and I notice some positive correlation between my degree of investment and theirs.

I don't pretend to be a scholar. Really I'm not a very scholarly person, although I do like to think about, read, and discuss vital issues related to psychology, education, philosophy, and other areas of humanism. While I am interested in current research in my field, I do not consider myself a scientific researcher in the strict sense of the term. I see myself much more as a practitioner, and the research I do conduct is directly related to studying the effectiveness of my classes and encounter groups as agents of change. Personally, I find it very difficult to be both teacher and researcher. My primary allegiance is to students, and I fear that if I become deeply engrossed in research projects my doors would not be open to students as they are now.

I have lost the desire to teach subject matter, present information, and do other professional things expected of a professor! I get bored by merely dispensing information. However, when I get wound up talking about some of my deepest feelings about education, I find not only that I enjoy this exposition, but that it generates lively debate and dialogue in the class.

While we are admonished to be objective and keep our bias out of our classroom, I prefer to state my bias publicly on the first day. I have some definite beliefs based upon examination and experience, and it seems to me a denial of my own identity to keep my personal bias out of this class.

I enjoy open debate in my classroom and encourage it. I would like to become more skillful at it than I now am. Too often I find students too frozen to get really involved in a debate—too paralyzed for fear of displeasing the teacher. I would like more dialogue in my class than now exists. Still too few actively participate, and I confess that so far I haven't discovered an effective way to have more participate. It seems that calling attention to nonparticipation causes the silent students to become more silent, more resistant, and more hostile. Others seem to comply and talk simply because of their need to give the professor what he wants.

I share my own struggles with my students. And I want to share with them some of my experiences in my past and present work as an educator, psychologist, and consultant for special projects. When it is appropriate, and when I care to, I share personal experiences as they are related to my life as a husband, father, learner, or whatever. I believe in the value of self-disclosure, although I admit that at times I find myself playing games, hiding behind roles, being defensive, manipulating, being phony, being nice to keep from offending and receiving disapproval. I don't like these traits when I discover them in myself, but I am becoming increasingly able to recognize them and to some extent accept them.

Surely one of my major problems is that in my love for what I am doing, I expect my students to evidence the same enthusiasm. While there is nothing wrong in wanting a class full of alive, dynamic students, I wish I could accept the reality that some (maybe many) simply do not care that much and are there merely to earn five required credits—as painlessly as possible with the smallest amount of personal expenditure.

I believe in granting freedom, and I attempt to release as many controls as students genuinely want. I like to grant freedom to students, but it means that students must take the initiative and accept responsibility for their own choices. A problem I have found is that students often interpret freedom to mean license to do nothing. Freedom is sometimes viewed as the absence of any structure, requirements, expectations, or demands. What I need to develop is the ability to endure the students' process of learning how to accept freedom, but right now I'm an impatient fellow in this regard.

In a classroom session, I will find myself challenging others at times, lecturing at other times, attempting to understand at other times, and often asking a seminar group to be aware of the process of what is going on *now* in the present group. I am striving to behave spontaneously instead of performing expected professional functions. This is difficult for me; in this regard, I am a slow learner.

I believe in open expression of both thought and feelings, an area where I find considerable resistance from students. I struggle with my feelings as students express their distrust of the procedures and processes in the class. Many have never experienced a classroom where they could (much less were expected to) disclose their views, values, thoughts, and feelings. Most have a difficult time in learning to share their feelings or opinions openly. Some resist because they fear their tricky psychologist-professor is attempting to "do psychotherapy" on them without their consent. Most express the wish that they could more actively express what they feel and think in our seminar sessions, but for so many years they have been accustomed to a vastly different role as a student that they are at a loss to know where to begin.

A special problem I wrestle with is that of time, number of students, and a vast amount of data to absorb, think about, evaluate, and integrate. The course I am describing meets for one quarter, about ten weeks of working time. It meets three times weekly for two hours. This means that we have sixty hours of class contact time, with forty students in a class. A real problem I have observed is that students do a vast amount of reading, of listening to speakers with various specialties, of participating in field work in schools, and of discussing their learnings both inside and outside of the classroom. There comes a saturation point where students tend to become confused and unclear as to the meaning of what they are experiencing. I do feel that insecurity, confusion, anxiety, and ambiguity are necessary for real learning, and I do not view this confusion as undesirable. At times, though, a student needs to stand back and assess what he is doing, why he is doing it, and where it is leading. Time is needed to integrate in one's being these subtle and new learnings. When students take four to six courses per quarter, this incubation period is often unavailable.

SOME OUTCOMES

In closing I want to mention some outcomes of this class, based largely upon student evaluation.

Most students have the initial experience of being overwhelmed —of feeling that they could never do all that is expected with one quarter. Many are genuinely excited by this approach, and most seem to respond by exerting far more effort than is minimally expected. Some students who take an active role in their learning really come to life. They fully give themselves to the challenges in the course and open themselves to serious self-examination.

Many students read more than one book a week. At first they are sure they will never read even one book; but as they get interested in the reading, they surprise themselves with the enjoyment they derive from reading. Some even admit to feeling guilty for enjoying their work!

Most rate the field work as an invaluable experience—often *the* most important and useful part of the course. Instead of merely meeting the minimum number of hours, most far exceed these hours once they feel personally involved.

I've found some students are bitter, hostile, closed, and suspicious. They can see no value in what we are doing. Some of these students complain that the course is negative in that it focuses upon what is wrong with education. Some want to be shown and told *how* to teach, and what to do when. . . . There are others that respond with genuine enthusiasm. First they become enraged when they become aware of what their schooling has done to them; later they become enthusiastic over the possibility of providing a different kind of learning for their own students.

I have administered anonymous questionnaires after each quarter, and in general, the results are encouraging. I have also sent follow-up open-ended questionnaires to the same students one year later. I asked them to respond to the lasting value and impact of this course upon them. Again, the response (over 50 percent) is mostly favorable and encouraging. But I wonder about that other 50 percent!

There is no real conclusion here. What I have attempted to do is to share with you some of my approach in attempting to assist teacher candidates to become more self-aware, to be more aware of some crucial issues they will eventually face, and to change in ways which to them seem constructive and growth-oriented. As I said earlier, I am experimenting, discovering mistakes, learning from my errors, and slowly encountering more effective ways of helping students to reach *themselves.* And this is precisely the challenge—to have the student reach himself, not the instructor reach the student!

7

Teachers Who Are Making a Difference

In this chapter, four teachers speak for themselves about their class-room procedures, their ways of preceiving students, their goals and ways of achieving them, and their evolution as teachers and persons. Each of these four teachers has been selected as an example of people who are practicing many of the principles discussed in this book. While none of these teachers view themselves as ideal, they have in common a quest for discovering more effective ways of reaching students and in significant ways are helping their students to find their own way as thinking and feeling persons. To provide a picture of what each of these teachers is like and how they operate in their classrooms, I have interviewed them separately and asked certain leading questions.

To give you a more comprehensive look at the effects these teachers are having upon their students, I developed a student evaluation form with fifteen open-ended questions and asked each teacher to have his students write anonymously how they felt about the teacher and the course. When the evaluations were completed I selected samples from several questions so you would have an opportunity to perceive each of these four teachers as their students do. I feel these student comments can stand alone, without explanation or discussion. The student comments were not changed, even for spelling, grammar, or punctuation.

As you read these interviews you will notice that each teacher represents a different field. In their own ways, which are the expression of their separate and distinct personalities, each teacher is showing that *change is possible*, that students do want to learn, and that students appreciate a teacher who creates a climate where real learning can occur. Most important of all, four teachers are living proof that a single teacher can reform and even revolutionize traditional education along humanistic lines. The teachers can dare to be people, without keeping the students at a distance. And this change of the classroom from a place of potential boredom to a place where real learning occurs can and does occur within the present system. Since many teachers have the defeatist attitude of "What's the use—change will never occur under the present system," we need a strong reminder: CONSTRUCTIVE CHANGE IS POSSIBLE WITHIN THE SYSTEM! These teachers give a ray of hope that reformation is possible—with exertion of effort and the courage to dare to be different.

AN INTERVIEW WITH PATRICIA DUNBRIDGE
FRENCH TEACHER
WALNUT HIGH SCHOOL, WALNUT, CALIFORNIA

Pat Dunbridge is the rare individual who can successfully combine learning with fun in the classroom. It is a delight to sit in her classroom and observe her naturalness, enthusiasm, and gusto for teaching. Here is a person who commands the genuine respect of her students by what she is in her class. While she relates with her students warmly and as a friend, the students give the impression that they know who is the teacher. As you read the section of student comments you will be able to sense what students really *want* in a teacher. I'm sure you will sense the love and respect they have for her. A point I would like to make is that Pat Dunbridge has worked hard at achieving this success; she continues in her struggles to become more effective, personally and professionally.

Pat is a young teacher with five years of teaching experience. I think her greatest asset as a French teacher is her vitality as a person. Her enthusiasm for French (and for most other things as well) is highly contagious. Here is an example of a humanistic class where students are valued as persons. Many of her aims (aside from teaching French) are done in a class that does not readily lend itself to discussion of human problems. And her students *do* learn French well; in fact many elect to take an extra year of French. For a clue as to why, read ahead.

JERRY COREY: Pat, besides teaching your students French, what else do you want to give your students? What do you hope they will leave your class with?

PAT DUNBRIDGE: This is really hard to explain, but I suppose I would very much like to give my students *me*, as a person—I would like to make myself known to them: my humanness, my struggles, my enthusiasm not only for teaching and for French but for life itself. I would like to offer them friendship. I'm not speaking of a palsy-walsy relationship here. Rather, I would like to think that they would feel comfortable with me as a person and that they would sense that I would understand them, their problems, worries, and fears. I would also like to give them some of my openness to new experiences and feelings—a willingness to take risks and thereby live life more freely.

I would like them to leave my class with love and respect for me as an individual, love and respect not built on fear of my authority over them, but built on a foundation of trust and understanding which we have constructed together over a period of time. Based on their experience in my class, I would hope that, in a broader sense, they would also leave my class loving life more than they did before, with less fears and more trust in themselves and in others.

JERRY: Would you say a few words on how you view your students? How do you relate to them, and how do you treat them?

PAT: I love my students. I have often thought that, given a choice of being with a group of typical teachers and being with a group of students, I would, without hesitation, pick the latter. Adolescents are a wonderful group to relate to—they are open and honest and direct. If they like you, they cannot pretend otherwise—nor do they seem to feel it makes them vulnerable, as so many adults do, to tell you of their feelings. The same can be said if they dislike you and what you are doing. I guess they don't play as many games in order to relate to others as most adults find necessary to do in order to survive.

I'm not saying I love all of my students equally. They are definitely individuals; some I like better than others; a few I dislike. But as a group, I find them delightful. I love being with them.

I don't find it necessary to talk down to my students, nor do I try to be "one of them." On the other hand, I don't place myself above them with a kind of professional attitude—me, teacher; you, peon. I suppose the best way to describe how I relate to my students is that I'm just me. I don't pretend to be anything I'm not. I think I'm pretty much the same person inside the classroom and out. I treat my students as I would treat anyone—"This is me. I am not going to play any role for you. That would be too easy for both of us."

I have broken down and cried once or twice in front of classes, experienced and shown elation and also anger. I find my students, without exception thus far, have been able to deal with my exposure of myself to them. And, I think they love me all the more for it.

JERRY: For you, what are the rewards of teaching? What do you get from your students and from your work?

PAT: For me, the rewards of teaching are so numerous, that I think I could spend hours listing them. Instead, I'll try to cite a few of what I consider to be the most important. For one, I think I'm a natural ham, and I just eat up any opportunity to exercise this facet of my personality—and what better occasion than the classroom! There I can demonstrate my nutty side to its fullest extent, with a captive audience to appreciate me! And appreciate, they do. I can tell that they enjoy *my* enjoying myself—so I guess it's a mutually rewarding experience.

Another reward for me is when suddenly my students discover they know French—either by placing high on a college entrance achievement exam, or more significant, I feel, after having been placed in a position where they were required to communicate and comprehend the language, and succeeding! That really makes me feel proud and gives me a tremendous sense of accomplishment.

Furthermore, it is extremely rewarding to be well thought of by my colleagues and my principal. To be regarded by these people as an outstanding teacher is, without a doubt, extremely satisfying and gratifying to me.

Finally, I think most significant of all the rewards of teaching for me, is the feeling of love that I receive from my students. I can see it in their eyes, the way they speak to me, the way they wish to continue to have something with me as a person even after I am no longer their French teacher, the way they feel free to visit with me, how they confide in me as a friend, and when they turn to me in trust and confidence for advice or just for a sympathetic ear. *That*, Jerry, is the greatest reward of teaching.

JERRY: Could you say something about how you structure your class?

What are some of the ways you try to make learning French more exciting?

PAT: Being a foreign language class, French demands more structure than, for example, English or social science. There is no getting around the fact that I have certain knowledge to impart to my students, moving from simple phrases and sentences to more complex ideas and expressions.

Still, I firmly believe that learning can and should be fun. I try to use the structure to aid me, rather than allow myself to be caught up in a dull and rigid routine. I try to sense when the students are becoming tired of an activity (it's usually the same time I'm beginning to get bored) and stop it. Why make learning a torturous ordeal?

Any time a student asks an intelligent question, regardless of whether or not it is "relevant to the material being studied" at the time, I answer it. As a result, my structure is always flexible. We often digress to subjects other than French, but I still feel real learning is going on at these times. I really think that if a student is curious enough to ask a thought-provoking question, he deserves an answer.

Getting back to the concept that learning should be fun, it never ceases to amaze me how many students think that they've got to be miserable if they're learning something. They are usually surprised if, after a fun day in class, they come to the realization that they actually learned quite a bit!

We play games in French in order to try and make the class more fun and exciting. I use games such as Bingo and Hangman and French Relay Races at the elementary level to 20 Questions and awareness activities at the advanced levels. By awareness acivities, I'm referring to Trust Walks and fantasizing seeing oneself in front of a mirror (all done in French).

We go caroling at Christmas time, have a visit to a French restaurant once a year, look at slides of Europe, see French films, experiment tasting different French foods, and generally have a pretty good time together.

JERRY: Do you allow time for activities other than teaching French? Do you often encourage students to talk about themselves, their feelings? Can you accomplish both goals?

PAT: Yes, I do allow for things besides French, although I prefer to consider it *making* time for these activities when the situation presents itself. Rarely do I plan for these activities in advance. Instead, I try to have a spontaneous and flexible classroom. I have discovered that when *I'm* not in the mood to teach it, that there's no use forcing it.

It also seems that because we do things other than the same old cut-and-dried routine of sticking to the book each and every minute of each and every day, the students are much more responsive and receptive to French when we work on the language. This is probably because they *want* to work on French and also because they consider the other discussions and activities we do to be privileges. This encourages them to try harder to pick up French so they can have time for other things.

We often talk about our feelings—theirs and mine. After a while, many of them open up and discuss themselves; sometimes we discuss the class itself; more often than not, we'll get onto some pretty heavy discussions about personal problems, politics, and life. No answers are given, but more and more possibilities are explored which usually lead to greater self-examination and sometimes (hopefully) greater self-awareness on my part and on the students' parts. On the advanced level, we attempt to do this in French much of the time. When the discussion becomes pretty heavy, we often go back to English, but I feel the experience is nevertheless very worthwhile.

Most of my students complain that they don't really have the opportunity to express themselves and their feelings in other classes. This makes them feel rather closed in and gives them the impression that their teachers don't really have any interest in them as people. They really need to be recognized as individuals and to express themselves, to ask questions, to explore their feelings. This to me is as important, if not more important, than the simple teaching of French.

JERRY: Do you have much contact with your students outside of class? From what your students say, it seems that they consider you as both a friend and a counselor, in addition to an effective French teacher. What kinds of problems do you deal with outside of class? How do you attempt to help?

PAT: I have an awful lot of contact with my students outside of class. This is of my own choosing. I encourage students to come and see me to talk about French or anything they want to discuss. I enjoy their company and the chance to get to know them outside of the classroom environment.

I don't encourage a real buddy-buddy type of relationship with them because I don't think that's what either of us wants. Most of the time they aren't looking for a pal but for someone to talk to. They need to know their teachers are concerned about them as individuals. Very often they are amazed to discover that we have a lot in common—music, movies, dancing, attitudes about life and about ourselves. We may even be struggling with the same things!

I don't always deal with problems. Often students drop into my office to tell me about something they're really happy about—they're eager to share their joy and enthusiasm. But often students with problems come for counseling or just a shoulder to cry on. I've dealt with problems such as pregnancy, drugs, inability to get along with a parent or parents, being beaten up by other kids or parents, running away from home, boyfriend or girlfriend problems, personality conflicts with siblings and friends. When confronted with problems such as these, I really struggle with the urge to tell the kid what *I* think he should do. I don't think it's right to impose my prejudices and attitudes on students, even though I do know sometimes I can't help but do that. When that happens I tell the student that I am biased on the subject—I think that's only fair to them.

Ideally, I make an effort to listen, to understand, and if desired by the student, to give as many alternatives as I can think of for his situation so that he has a choice. I try to discourage them from any rash actions without considerable thought.

Jerry: What do you feel that students today really want from their teachers? What kind of teacher do you see as reaching and touching the lives of their students in a significant way?

Pat: Most of all, I feel the students want authenticity from their teachers. They want to relate to their teacher as a real person, not as some machine or as some role-playing human being standing up there. If they feel their teacher is sincere and real, then they will open themselves up to learning, to building a relationship, and to self-examination. But they must first identify with the teacher as a person. They appreciate the reality that differences do and must exist between them and the teacher—this must be the case when a teacher tries to be cool, to be "hip," and it's just an act, just another role. They just want their teacher to be himself.

Students also badly want friendship and understanding from a teacher—someone to rap with—someone who will listen and hopefully understand. They don't necessarily want to be "yes'd" all the time; I think it's mostly having an adult who will listen and try to be objective.

Finally, students really *want to learn*. I think sometimes we tend to forget that. But it's probably the most important. They want to learn the subject, they want to learn about life, and they want to learn about themselves. And it's the teachers' responsibility to provide an environment where such learning can take place. Never do you hear a more bitter or more resentful comment from a student than, "Boy,

I sure hated that class! We never did anything in there. We never learned a thing. It was a useless waste of time!"

I would hope that a student who took some of my classes would say, "I learned a lot of French and I also learned many other important things along with it."

JERRY: Do you feel it is important to let students know you as a person? Should a teacher disclose his or her feelings to a class? How much of yourself do you choose to share with your students, and what is the impact upon them of your sharing?

PAT: I share practically all of myself with my students. It's impossible for me to draw some sort of a line, i.e., this is the extent to which I shall reveal my true self in class. Impossible, really! I'm the same in class as out of class. This doesn't make me feel vulnerable at all. I feel that because my students know me well, they have more feelings for me. This is perhaps the reason why I have so many students coming to me for counseling—because they feel I can identify with their problems. After all, I have feelings too. I get depressed, angry, exuberant, overjoyed. Since I communicate these feelings to my students, I guess they all feel I can better understand theirs.

When they share certain things they are struggling with, I often share some of the problems I'm dealing with. This is good for me, and it's good for them, too. It lets them know teachers struggle with problems, too.

Some students don't really see teachers as being human at all. They don't have problems. They don't have feelings—they probably never do anything that real people do, like smoke or drink or have sex! Students see teachers like this because many teachers don't let their students know them—they are afraid to share their feelings, afraid of being taken advantage of, I suppose.

I would like to say here that *never* in my five years of teaching have I had my openness with students backfire on me. Rather, it has worked to my advantage in establishing a beautiful rapport between my students and me.

JERRY: Your students feel that you genuinely trust them, and they add that they feel real freedom to be themselves in your class. How do you create this climate of trust? Do you feel that most students can creatively handle freedom?

PAT: I don't think I consciously create a climate of trust in my class. Actually, if I were to make up my own questions for a student evaluation of me as a teacher, I don't believe I'd even think of asking the question, "Do you feel your teacher trusts your class?" What I'm trying to say is, trust comes naturally to me. I tend to be trusting of people in general and also trusting of my feelings. Since I'm not a different person in the classroom from out, I naturally trust my students.

What I never expected was how much my students indicated they appreciated the trust I place in them. It is evidently a very valuable thing, and many have indicated they never do anything to jeopardize that trust.

I think it all boils down to how a person sees man's basic nature. If one feels that man is basically evil, then as a teacher this person will *expect* a class to be malicious, to try to get to the teacher, to cheat, to create discipline problems, etc. And I really think that the kids sense this and will act according to the expectations of the teacher.

However, if the teacher believes as I do, that man is basically good, then they would expect that students would be able to handle trust, responsibility, and freedom. I have rarely been disappointed in this.

JERRY: Have you made any personal changes in your life that you feel have a direct relationship to your becoming a more effective teacher?
PAT: After four encounter groups and some individual psychotherapy for awhile, I should say so! To begin with, it was a big step for me to even become involved in therapy of any kind. I used to believe that one really had to be "sick" to need this kind of help, or that it was sort of a mark of weakness to admit that one was in therapy or had a "shrink." But now I really think that *everyone* could benefit from an encounter group experience or two. If you don't choose to become personally involved with your own feelings in a group, at least you can benefit from becoming more aware of other people and how they feel.

For me, I have become much more accepting as a result of my experiences in group and individual therapy. I actually like myself, the person I am and the person I'm becoming! Because of this, I can deal with other people, my students included of course, more honestly. You see, before I *needed* approval from others so badly that I would base all of my actions on getting that approval, always afraid of possibly alienating others if I said or did what I really wanted. Now, I have enough confidence in myself and my feelings to do and say what I really feel. And so, I'm more real with others. I've found this to be helpful in relating to my students, both on an individual basis and with my classes.

WHAT STUDENTS SAY ABOUT PATRICIA DUNBRIDGE AND HER FRENCH CLASS

These were replies submitted anonymously by Pat Dunbridge's students. Their statements appear as they were written and not corrected for grammar, spelling, or structure. They speak for themselves.

Question: How does it feel to be a student in this class?

Student Responses

- I'm proud to be one of Mrs. Dunbridge's students 'cause she's one of the coolest teachers at our school. She identifies with us but not so far that she makes us feel like she's trying to be something she's not. She compromises to give us what we need to learn and to give us what we *want* to learn.
- Really different. Because of Mrs. Dunbridges sense of humor, I actually *look forward* to this class, (don't tell anybody).
- Great. Fantastic. I love learning in this class and what I'm learning I'm learning in an atmosphere that mixes pleasure with work.
- I like this class. You can express your ideas and feelings. We have a very unique class, in that we learn a tremendous amount of French and we also learn a lot about each other and the world.
- I feel like I'm a human being. I'm not forced to sit and take everything in and give no comments. In this class the teacher listens to me and other students instead of cutting us off like in most my other classes. I'm not imprisoned in the class like an animal.
- It's neet because you don't feel so much like a *student*. You're trusted to do your work you're given a chance to learn responsibility and the subject. You don't have to be embarassed to ask the teacher about something—it's not a stiff atmosphere.
- To be a student in this class, you feel more mature. Many classes in this high school do not give you freedom. It's different in here. You can express anything you please. It doesn't have to relate to the class or what you are studying at the time.

Question: What do you like most about this class?

- I enjoy the relaxed atmosphere. You can be more yourself. I found that I can learn better in this type of atmosphere. Thats the best part—to know a class can be held relaxed and personal and learning can be carried on. It just goes to show that you don't have to have a dictatorship in the classroom.
- The class is conducted in a relaxed way. We may express ourselves when we feel like doing so. We arrange our desks in a circular way so that we all face one another. We work orally most of the time which I like very much. This is a good way of learning communication as well as French grammar.
- I like the *freeness* we have—like not getting in trouble for being

late—the ability to do things that you can't in other classes, no
permanent seats, talking and discussing the French without having
to raise your hand—the kind of relation we have—the class.

- I like the fact that Mrs. Dunbridge talks to the students on an equal
level. She doesn't *look down* on us . . . it's as though we're *people*
and not just objects to drill facts into. Another thing is that she's
not concerned with just the things we're supposed to know from
our texts. If we (the students) aren't in the mood to learn French,
then there is no reason to attempt to teach us. Mrs. Dunbridge
seems to realize this and she will let the line of conversation digress
from French. These things give Mrs. Dunbridge something a lot
of teacher don't have: *Our respect!*
- Both the language and Mrs. Dunbridge. I would not like French
half as much if she didn't teach us. She is a most enthusiastic
teacher which makes me *want* to learn it too.

*Question: Describe in your own words how you see your teacher? How do you
feel toward your teacher?*

- I see Mrs. Dunbridge as a beautiful, warm, understanding teacher.
She puts aside her personal feelings and moods for teaching. She
is very open and natural. This makes everyone else relaxed and
more willing to learn. She is very honest with us. I think everyone
in the class respects her, not because she is strickt, but because we
value her opinion.
- We were told to look at this evaluation honestly—no snow jobs.
I can honestly say that Mrs. Dunbridge is by far my favorite
teacher. She just seems to go overboard with enthusiasm, and she
really gets excited with her work. Outside the class she really cares
about the students. She even set aside her free period to be a
counseling service—kind of an Ann Landers.
- My teacher is personal, and yet can stop you at a glance. She has
total control over a class without coming on heavy.
- I have never met a more feeling person. She brings her self into
her teaching making us want to know her and learn.

*Question: What are some things about this class that are different from your
other classes?*

- The complete lack of inhabitions on the part of the instructor. You
can almost picture her authoring *The Senuous Woman* and yet like
Fanny Hill which contains not one obscene passage or gesture it
would probably to completely respectable. She can easily be seen
on her knees, praying for snake eyes while shooting craps as well
as listening to Michel Legrand's "I Will Wait for You" from "The
Umbrellas of Cherbourg." It is the utter lack of complete preten-
tiousness and the venerable facade.

- In most other classes there is a very definite separation between teachers and students. The teachers have the knowledge and we are the uninformed that must listen and learn. In French it is much more a team work. Mrs. Dunbridge does not act superior, yet she has respect. Her attitude is more like "I'm in here to share something I know with you."
- In this class your not isolated from emotions and feelings as you are in other classes. In this class nothing is fed to you from all one direction. You can reach out in this class for something anything —any need and not be afraid to be a human first—then a student.
- The class is well conducted, attentive, and thorough. The teacher handles it well and is able to keep control of it. The students are not treated like children, but as maturing young adults.
- The teacher talks to her class, she isn't a machine or a robot, very cold and impersonal. She can feel with us or for us.
- I like the teacher better. She acts like an equal, not like some who act better than the kids they teach.

Question: To what degree do you feel your teacher trusts your class?

- She trusts us very much, and she can too. Everyone respects her and there is no reason to do anything wrong. The kids would never think of doing anything to hurt her.
- I feel she trusts our class very much. She can depend on us to do our work and not have to warn us to not get into trouble. She feels we are responsible enough to conduct ourselves accordingly.
- She has an unbelievable amount of trust, this is very unusual situation. It gives students a sense of security and in turn trust. It is a great achievement for a teacher to gain this trust from a student.
- 100% We as a class respect her and she as a teacher respects us. So *I* feel!
- I think she trusts us a lot because she puts some responsibility on us and we don't want to let her down because we want her to trust us.

Two students chose to ignore the structured evaluation form I provided, and wrote their own essays on what the French class meant to them. Their responses are presented below:

To be a student in this class is to be a part of a whole, yet keeping your individuality. This is the only class in which I have been able to feel a close relationship among everyone, particularly I believe because of its small size. The whole class is made up of quite different people who pool their efforts together to make a closely-knit group, with all our ideas and undertaken projects made successful. Never have I had a class, with an exception of one perhaps where there is no real definite classroom routine to be followed each day—unfaltering. If someone in the class has a problem to share we abandon our books for the day and all gather in a circle, expressing our ideas and feelings. Each person learns to accept the other people and himself. I believe I have benefitted more greatly from this experience than I would've had we just kept up a regular routine in the class. This free-feeling atmosphere has made it more enjoyable for learning French and her methods of teaching are so bubbly and well-planned, it becomes a lot of fun to learn it. However being a French 4 I'm in independent study which in itself is a good thing, but I don't get to be as much a part of the class as I would like. Mrs. Dunbridge is one exceptional teacher and I would like to be under her instruction a little more. I can relate to her as a friend in many ways because she is easy to talk to. She can understand how you feel, but she still presents the other side of the situation to make you think about it more clearly. I believe Mrs. Dunbridge sees the class much as we feel, individuals making up a unique group. I've been in several of her classes for 3 years, and she treats each of them in a special way according to their composition. The further up the line you go the more lenient and informal the class becomes. Some of the really different things about this class are things we do. Instead of just learning the language out of a textbook, we learn the culture by going to a French restaurant, a French play, and making our own restaurant menu and all—even food. People who normally wouldn't care about school participate and become enthused. These extra things we have planned and successfully done have made this class one of my most rewarding. I wanted mostly to learn to speak French, and although I've progressed much farther than I would have in another high school class, I still have a lot more to learn. It's not what I planned to learn, so much as what I have learned unexpectantly, an understanding for all people has deepened. Its hard to say with all the advantages in this class what I would change. I feel Mrs. Dunbridge in allowing ourselves to speak freely and treating us as adults, yet not losing the fun of youth, gives us a considerable amount of trust.

● ● ●

The first thing that attracted me to this teacher was her magnetic charm and her overwhelming enthusiasm. She is definitely the most vavacious, alive, and bubbly teacher I have ever seen in front of a classroom.

There is one word that perfectly describes Mrs. D. as a teacher. In her teacher-role as in many other of her roles, she is best known as playful. She creates an atmosphere in the classroom that is vividly reminiscent of one's childhood. She enjoys "playing." She loves to

compose games for her students. Yet the beautiful part of her childhood classroom is that not only does she create an atmosphere which
plunges each student backward into time, but she herself goes backward with us. That is to say that she does not allow herself to look
down at us, i.e. viewing us as children—but she puts herself on the
same level. I imagine the reason I always think of this class atmosphere as child-like is because everything is run on emotion. Mrs. D.
relies so greatly on insight. She can feel with her heart the things she
needs to know in order to better teach. She is the most perceptive
teacher I've ever known. I love her because she is so unpragmatic.
She realizes her students are susceptible to emotions, being human;
and whenever one of her students has a problem, she is extremely
perceptive to it. She takes class time to talk to the student about his
problem and she allows other students to talk and discuss and they
try to help as peers. She makes the students feel that they are more
important than the learning of French. She has always been an intensely considerate and concerned teacher. All of her students know
she is available to talk whenever they need her and many feel completely free and at ease to talk with her about anything. She has the
remarkable talent as a teacher to be able to look at her students eye
to eye at the same level and yet her students look up to her.

The outstanding teaching ability of Mrs. D. is essentially at-
tributed to the type of person she is. She is very open-minded and
willing to respect and listen to each opinion presented to her. The
students sense this and are not afraid to open up to her. She gives
each student a feeling of importance and worth and students need
that feeling especially at this time of their lives when they begin to
feel surpressed. But every person needs to feel that what they have
to say is important not only those in my age bracket.

The best type of teacher is he who develops his students mind and
makes the student believe he has a right to think what he wants, and
the only truths are those which are truths for himself.

"If a teacher is indeed wise, he does not lead a student to the house
of wisdom, but rather to the threshold of his own mind."

AN INTERVIEW WITH DICK NEWTON
TEACHER OF MODERN LITERATURE
WHITTIER HIGH SCHOOL, WHITTIER, CALIFORNIA

In my first job as a public high school teacher at Whittier High
School, I met a person who taught me a great deal, not only about
teaching, but about life as well. After school on Fridays at the local
beer joint, Dick Newton challenged many of my rigid ideas and helped

me to see that there were more sides to an issue than I was willing to examine. For almost twenty years now, Dick Newton has been at Whittier High School; and his classes have been modified considerably during these years. When I was on the staff there I used to hear students say, "I hated English until I got Newt, and now I even dig poetry. Newt really knows how to turn us on to reading."

Dick Newton does not present himself to his students as a supremely well-adjusted person; rather he shares his own problems, his past failures and his present struggles. He relates to students in much the same way as he relates to adults. Students know where they stand with him.

I think Dick has been particularly successful in reaching students who are given labels such as slow, unmotivated, reluctant learners, and academically untalented. He has a real talent for integrating what is current in the lives of young people with the academic pursuit of learning to read and appreciate contemporary literature. I respect Dick for what he is able to give his students, and many ex-students return years later to let Newt know that he *did* make a difference in their lives.

That meaningful change can occur *within* the present educational system is evidenced by the work of Dick Newton. He deeply believes that he can learn from his students, and he feels they keep him contemporary. However, as a member of the "Establishment," he feels he can offer young people ideas from his own experiences. He truly tries and succeeds in bridging the gap between the generations in his classroom.

JERRY COREY: Dick, you've been teaching at Whittier High School now for over twenty years. Could you share with us how you feel you have changed with respect to the way you view your function as a teacher? How have you evolved to become the teacher you are now?

DICK NEWTON: In the initial period of my career, I was trying to find an area in which to teach. Having jumped from physical education to speech to drama to remedial instruction left me rather confused. I just didn't feel as though I had found and developed my self strongly and in a most involved way in an academic field. I guess I felt that my entire program was mostly a personality approach to the students but limited in real materials the teacher respected!

Always I have gotten along well with the students and have tried to be most understanding, because I care about others. The big difference in the last ten years has been that I feel I have more to offer the student, because when I ran into the field of reading and relating, I knew more about what Gibran says in his poetry relative to work being love that is made viable. Before I liked—later I loved—probably because I had given myself more. It just might be self-confidence and the desire to get better.

JERRY: Dick, it might be helpful to give us a general picture of what your modern literature class is like. What are the goals you have? What kinds of topics and issues are discussed?

DICK: Modern Lit. is set up much like a buffet with many offerings for each student. The choice factor, the lack of pressure, the organized but free-flowing program—all these provide an atmosphere for all to do something that makes sense. Although most do something meaningful, many don't. Like any program, there are those who just don't, but unlike most programs, those who do really can take fire and some who don't or can't respond in a heavier program find that there is no great pressure to compete against anyone but themselves.

I feel that a heterogeneous class with all kinds of backgrounds, reading experiences, and levels of learning makes for the good environment. With self-evaluations, little pressure in terms of grades, and seminars that grow from their interest and desires while at the same time book lists that are made up by the teacher and/or the student on an individual basis helps to motivate them where the textbook could kill off the program.

My philosophy is that the teacher should have much care, give buckets of understanding by listening and watching well and just not be an obstacle to learning.

JERRY: What do the students *do* in your Modern Literature class? What do you do? How do you see your function?

DICK: The students do some things together such as rap sessions on race, generation, parents, war, religion, existentialism, drugs, etc. They work separately on individual projects ranging from reading in astronomy (building a telescope) to pleasure reading books at the fourth-grade level.

Many utilized the community for future vocational development, people, interest things, and an exposure to the practical aspect of things. The classroom is but a spring-board for some. For example, a student may read modern literature, study nursing, while another may read in the medical field and for pleasure read *Temple of Gold* by William Goldman. We just try to get those who aren't interested to become involved, to branch out.

The teaching approach is one of being a resource person, counselor, and behind-the-scenes manager of the whole merry-go-round. The art of questioning (Socratic) and suggestion helps the students to help themselves.

JERRY: As you see it, Dick, what is some distinctive feature of your program? In what ways is your modern literature class different and unique? What are some of the most exciting things you've done in class lately?

DICK: The most unique quality is the rapport factor. We are so that we can trust each other by risking. Good teaching is dangerous as we must do some trusting and overlook many small things to give the student time and comfort to make changes, adjust, and get started.

In terms of our classes each individual is given time in consultation with the teacher about his program and/or himself. This takes much organization and energy and patience on the part of the teacher. At first they seem to treat the great amount of trust, sincerity, and freedom of choice with suspicion. In time the majority like it so well and move so smoothly at their own level that they take pretty good care of a good thing—not all but most!

The most exciting things have been seeing a nonreader read with such zest and go on to finish college and teach literature. Also to find many students reaching out, getting involved in ideas and people—in addition being associated with so many kids of different levels who seem to gain so much so soon emotionally and intellectually.

JERRY: Later we'll hear from your students directly, but could you say a few words how *you* feel your students respond to your program? Do they all become turned on? Do you have students who simply don't get involved in the program?

DICK: No group has all turned-on members; they are a very selective group and/or quite small in teacher–student ratio. Other than my Chicano Title I class, the classes are in the forties in size and thus the program is most difficult to manage. Most of the students are interested—do well in completing their contracts. Others can't handle the freedom and about the same number don't want the freedom. They want more structuring, so I give it to them even to the point of checking out a textbook, providing they will compromise with a bit of creativity thrown in to give things balance.

We don't have many disciplinary problems but some simply don't try, can't find or won't persist in finding at least something good on the buffet.

Last week I got a letter from a student who had been out of school for five years. Only now has she begun to do some of the things in our program, especially reading and relating with others. At least what was done must have been of some importance. Who can really tell what one learns but the student, if at all?

JERRY: Maybe you can say a few words about the frustrations you face as a teacher? What struggles do you have as a teacher? Are there some areas you are still working on?

DICK: Several of the frustrations I face are self-imposed due to a life of ups and downs. Although I seem to have a temperament somewhat like a yo-yo, I have mostly always felt best at school and least temperamental. I guess I must feel less threatened by younger people, for I have enjoyed them a good portion of time without the fears many teachers face.

Trying to keep some of my domestic problems in control after a death of one wife and a divorce with a second that in all includes three children's lives has been hard for me.

The difficulty at school is trying to do so many things to the point that in order to do them one sometimes just circumvents the system. Having a good administration has been a real help in keeping problems at a minimum. Although for years I used to teach books, invite speakers, and have seminars that could be and were in suspect with the parents, administration, and some faculty members. Good teaching is dangerous!

JERRY: Could you give us some ideas concerning your approach, methods, and special techniques? What are some ways of teaching that you have developed that seem particularly suited to your own style and personality?

DICK: 1. We begin all courses with one-to-one and small group rap sessions on all kinds of emotional, social, and intellectual ideas that will help each student to become more aware of others and of himself in the environment with so many different levels of others. These continue throughout the program.

2. Each student has a separate book list, vocational project (law, medicine, social worker, scientist, psychologist, automobile mechanics, etc.), or idea factory in which he can participate. Some reading and writing for most is part of the program.

3. The class is used to get students involved in community projects (tutoring, church work, counseling center, interviews with authors, poets, bookstore owner, professionals, college campus units, etc.) that will follow study in one of these fields. This is not a requirement as there are really few pressures.

4. Each student evaluates himself as to attitude, reading materials, relationships, etc. Also he evaluates the class and teacher.

5. Each student records and organizes his program in a way that is unique for him.

JERRY: From your experience, what do you see that students really need from teachers? What do they most need from their school experience?

DICK: I feel that the teacher's position is not to teach but to educate in any way that he can. He must not be an obstacle to learning.

Today the students need not a freezing mind or one that is so open nothing can stick and anything goes. No, the students need a teacher who will let the child come out himself, keep fear of failure at a minimum, and just try to experiment and to adjust and to enjoy what's happening. Sometimes just listening is the day's most profound lecture. Being there before and after school is really important, but being there as you are needed is the most important part we can play!

JERRY: As you see it, what are the characteristics of a teacher who truly *does* make a difference in the lives of students? What is an outstanding teacher?

DICK: Without checking a textbook or a class in Secondary principles, I feel that the following are mostly necessary:

1. Self-awareness (you)
2. Environmental awareness (others)
3. Being practical (changing/adjusting)
4. Dedication (being involved)
5. Being inspirational (awakening interest)
6. Being an example (hardest for me at times to be human and yet categorized with the role of a teacher)

JERRY: Would you care to share with us some of your own experiences as a student? Perhaps you can say something about why you decided to become a teacher.

DICK: As a student I was frustrated, in conflict much of school with myself and others, and not worth a damn as a student academically.

Having thrown education to the four winds and my life with it at times, the savior who helped me to find some grace under pressure was a track coach in high school. His example certainly triggered in me a desire to get through school in order to coach and help myself and others.

My guideline today is to teach as I have been taught. Most of the characteristics are part of my personality—being where some have put me in image does put a burden on me at times! I guess to be honest, they sometimes think more of me than I think of me. This I am working on although it is a tough road and one not enough well-travelled.

WHAT STUDENTS SAY ABOUT RICHARD NEWTON AND HIS ENGLISH CLASS

Question: How does it feel to be a student in this class?

Student Responses

- For most students this is the first class they have ever been in where they are given greater freedom at the price of respecting greater responsibility. I liked being in this class because of the greater freedom, but sometimes I felt I wasn't respecting my greater responsibility.

- I liked the freedom and responsibility it gave me. It's nice not having a step-by-step class.
- This class has been one of the few really enjoyable ones I've had. Unlike most classes a person is expected to do his own thing and after all, that's what we're going to have to do.
- Very different from the beginning of this class. I have a new attitude toward reading different books.
- I feel independent and it makes me feel that I'm being trusted. It has given me more responsiblity.
- It makes me feel as a student that I don't mind coming to this class. This class has a totally different atmosphere about it, a more relaxed class where things aren't pressed into your head. I have enjoyed this class every minute of it and wish it was for the whole year.
- I felt very well in this class. It helped me with some of my emotional problems. Also I feel I have gone much further than I would in a text-book class since I was allowed to choose my own reading program.
- Fantastic! It's so different from anything I've ever had that it's a welcome and refreshing class.

Question: What do you most like about this class?

- The idea of being able to choose *what* you want to learn about. (within the boundaries of the class.) The loose structure—you are your own person (self discipline).
- It's freeness and honesty. No one was afraid to say what he or she thought. Also, I liked the individual attention given to each student on his own level.
- *You*, Mr. Newton!
- The freedom you enjoy and the liberal selection of guest speakers. The guest speakers I enjoyed alot because I got a chance to talk to people I might have to talk to late in life.
- I like the freedom of being on my own. I can be more independent. You can read books at your own pace. I like the seminars. You can do your own kind of book reports.

Question: Describe in your own words how you see your teacher. How do you feel toward your teacher?

- Fig Newton is a man who cares for/about kids. He tries to do his best; the student, hopefully, becomes motivated. Fig tries; I admire anyone who puts forth effort.

- I feel comfortable around Mr. Newton because he gave me self-confidence. I learned that I was actually able to write well.
- I think Mr. Newton is a real cool guy. I have alot of respect for him. He shows that he cares about his students. I really like him alot. I wish more teachers were like him.
- I think our teacher has guts. It must take alot of nerve for him to give the students as much freedom as he has given us. I think he is the best teacher I've ever had.
- I feel that I can be honest with him and that he is honest with me. I can confide in him more than I can my other teachers.
- I think he has a very hard time in a class like this. However, he has more time to devote to individuals and he is not only helping us with our education, but also with our emotional, personal, family, etc. problems.
- I see a teacher that is trying very hard, but hasn't really got it all together yet. But what he is trying he is earnest in and I'm sure is the best way. He is a caring person, but I don't think I know him *at all.*
- I see my teacher as real, human being with hang-ups just like ours. Not a person up on a pedestal who I worship and cannot speak to. It's nice to have a teacher who will level with you and not pretend that he's superman, all great!
- Mr. Newton is so wrapped up in so many people it's amazing he hasn't gone crazy. I like the teacher quite a bit and respect the job he does.
- A fantastic leader. He gives us an incentive. "I love him" are the only words that can express my feeling.
- He doesn't pretend to be someone he's not. Some teachers try to play the role of all-knowing dictator. Mr. Newton is just a person like each of us and he's not afraid to show it. He's honest and he cares about each one of his students. He sincerely tries to do what he feels is right.

Question: How do you feel your teacher sees you as a class?

- As a group of people willing to learn but not knowing how. His task then is to "teach" or "show" us how.
- He thinks of us as people looking toward a goal and he's one of the "street signs" along the way.
- I can tell he enjoys teaching because he shows it by the way he talks.
- I think he really enjoys teaching. That's good, because so many teachers do just what they *have* to do and don't care about the kids.

Question: What are some things about this class that are different from your other classes?

- Your work is not forced upon you as in other classes. He lets you know how important it is but does not force or threaten anything. You become aware of your need yourself. Also he trusts us very much. We are very independent. Free from being tied down to regular class routine.
- You can work at your own pace and you aren't expected to react towards something if you don't want to talk. You are given the responsibility of thinking instead of have your "teacher" interpret things for you.
- There is more freedom to be yourself and the class is more directed toward wisdom rather than knowledge.
- The freedom. The relaxation. The responsibility. This class is preparing you for when you graduate and are out of high school. None of my other classes have ever done this.

Question: What are some of the most exciting and rewarding things you've done in the class so far?

- Reading books about life and love. Listening to seminars on love and marriage.
- The most "rewarding" thing was having time to read and enjoy books that I probably wouldn't have time for if I didn't have this class.
- I've begun to realize the exciting aspects of delving into literature for the depth and the hidden maxims. My writing has greatly improved and I've become secure in myself through my progression in the writing field.
- Raised my writings from *C-* to *A* and have seen my progress. Discussed me as a person and found understanding and similar feelings.
- The most rewarding thing is that I have gained a friend in a teacher whom I feel I can turn to.
- I've read *Siddhartha* and *Demian*—two of the greatest books ever written. I've worked harder on a written project than ever before, and I've had a chance to hear many people's views on many things!
- One of the seminars helped me find something in life that I had lost. After that my attitude toward the class and my life changed.
- The most rewarding thing was finding that I really *enjoy* reading and want to continue.
- Doing my own photography and writing my own poetry. Both have helped me to see inside of myself.

Question: Please use the rest of the space to write any comments you have about this class, the teacher, or any observations you care to make.

- I found out who I am and it feels great. I was with a great man for two years who is the best teacher I have ever had. I love you, Mr. Newton.
- Mr. Newton had the ability to create an atmosphere of mutual trust and respect. This is very important to students since not many people are able to do this.
- I have enjoyed this class more than any other I've ever had. Through writing, I have found a new way to better express myself. As a teacher, you're great, as a person, I feel very close. Thank you for your trust.
- I'll miss you, Mr. Newton.
- Mr. Newton as a teacher gives too much and tries too hard to help those who don't care. He doesn't get back half of what he gives but that makes him a truly outstanding human being. Thank you for all.
- Mr. Newton, You have always been here when I needed you. Thank you.

AN INTERVIEW WITH LINDA SCHNEIDER
HUMAN RELATIONS TEACHER
ALTA LOMA HIGH SCHOOL
ALTA LOMA, CALIFORNIA

In the picture on the next page, it's hard to tell who is the teacher and who are the students. Linda Schneider, the woman in the center, is a young teacher with young ideas. While I would not label her as a "radical," I do see her as a person who is affecting revolutionary changes in her classroom by working within the system. She knows what she really wants to accomplish as a teacher, and she is most willing to work instead of complain and ready to fight courageously for what she considers a good program for students.

As you will see in the interview, Linda Schneider developed a unique course aimed specifically at helping young people learn more about themselves, others, and crucial personal issues facing contemporary youth. While her class—human relations—deals with controversial issues, she has managed to sell her administration and the community on the need for this type of class. As you will read in the student

evaluation section, her students are also sold on her program. During the past two years Linda and many of her students came to my teacher preparation classes at California State Polytechnic University at Pomona and spent the day interacting with these future teachers. My students were amazed at the degree of maturity, openness, and awareness that these high school students evidenced. I'm sure that part of this ability to hold their own with college students is due to a class like human relations where they are encouraged to actively initiate.

For a glimpse at Linda's classes and how her students appraise the experience, read on.

JERRY COREY: Linda, as a teacher of human relations, could you comment on what your course is like? What is the main purpose of the course, and how do you try to accomplish your objectives?

LINDA SCHNIEDER: Human Relations is a one-semester course offered to sophomores, juniors, and seniors. The course is primarily a personal awareness class aimed at helping students gain greater self-awareness and understanding of others. Human relations gives the student the opportunity to select with other students and the teacher the specific topics to be discussed and studied in class. It is a personal awareness class designed to study current social problems from a behavioral science viewpoint. It gives the student the opportunity to express his own feelings, ideas, and problems in open discussion. The class attempts to develop the students' ability to think creatively and to help him explore his own goals, values, obligations to self and society. An important goal is that through this process of discussing and analyzing the student will become more sensitive, compassionate, and aware of the behavior of others as well as self-actualizing.

The structure of the class is provided from student–student–teacher planning into the areas of interest the class has. We plan not only one curriculum but also many of the (learning) activities that go on in the class. The students assume responsibility for providing speakers, films, outside field trips, daily content, for example. We have no desks in the room, but rather tables and chairs. We also have provided a couch and chairs that make up a reading area or a small discussion area.

My role of teacher is not to give directions and assignments but to provide the direction necessary and structure resources to make the program run smoothly so that what the students want to happen happens. I assume the role of learner along with my students. The class has many open discussions on topics of interest on large and small groups. From this discussion the class comes up with questions, problems, or other areas of concern they want to pursue further. From this we plan class activities and assignments that will help us reach our goals and objectives (help us answer our own questions). The student needs are considered in three ways in assignments. A student who needs structure gets it, although he is encouraged to become creative and make decisions for himself. By this a student who wants the structure has specific assignments, readings, and work-due dates. The student who is beginning to have self-direction has the same due dates but decides on his own assignments, projects, reading, etc. The student who can handle no structure on assignments makes up his own program complete with due dates, type of assignments, reading, etc. This is just an example of how things work in the class or how to get things working.

JERRY: What are some of the topics, questions, and issues you and your class explored during this semester?

LINDA: The students are mostly interested in understanding their own behavior—Who am I? Why do people do the things they do? The students are interested in learning about and how to deal with problems they are faced with in their own life. These problem areas are sex, drugs, getting along better with parents, communication, making the world a better place to live, how to be happy, and how to cope with problems.

JERRY: How do you see your function as different from that of a conventional teacher?

LINDA: To me a conventional teacher has a curriculum outline complete with behavioral objectives, goals, daily lesson plans, and student assignments. Much of the learning is from books and questions at the end of the chapter, with emphasis on thinkng and not feeling.

I do have objectives, but they are not necessarily mine. They are made up from student effort based on what they need and want from the class. We plan our lessons together and both student and teacher are responsible for what goes on in the classroom. Too, our classroom is not always within the boundaries of the school. We go out into the community to find out answers to what we want to know.

I hold the student responsible for his own behavior and when he breaks school or class rules, he is obligated to give reasons for such behavior and to change his behavior toward more positive behavior.

It is very important for me that my students know that I care for them in an *individual* way. To accomplish this I have not assumed the authoritarian role of teacher but rather have tried to establish a relationship of trust and respect with my students.

JERRY: What kind of reactions do you have toward many of your classes at the beginning of the semester? How about your reactions toward the end of the course? What kinds of changes do you notice in your classes?

LINDA: As we begin the semester, the students are not sure of their roles in the class and I find that I am often *frustrated!* This is because the students are not used to a class structured like human relations. They are more used to being told what to do and how to do it. In this class they have to assume more responsibility than they have assumed in many classes where the teacher assumes the task of curriculum planning without student involvement. As the students begin to believe that they do have a class where they can pursue learning into areas of their own interest, they assume the responsibility of planning and get involved to the point that in many classes I am no longer needed!

JERRY: Since your human relations course is controversial, how did you manage to make it a part of the curriculum at your school? What kinds of things did you actually do to make it come a reality?

LINDA: To establish a human relations course at my high school, I first conducted a student survey to show that there was a need for a class such as this—a class that helped students answer questions they have about their own growth and behavior and the behavior of others.

I wrote the class using the structure and framework utilized in my district—complete with curriculum outline and behavioral objectives. This was presented to my school principal and local curriculum committee for acceptance. I attended this meeting to assure all present that we would not have the community up in arms because of the "touchy" nature of the class and topics I assumed would be covered from information I had obtained from the student survey.

It was suggested by this committee that I start slowly into "touchy" areas of the class adding more each year as the class got accepted by the community (parents). By touchy areas, this implies sex, homosexuality, abortion, etc. . . . . areas that are highly emotional and diversified in any community.

I assured the curriculum committee that the class would not be the preaching sort that would put forth one way to believe or one answer to a problem but rather would be a class that would explore all answers and let the student choose the one he feels best fits into his own philosophy.

Parent permission would be a necessity for a class of this type, because I felt that for the class to really be worthwhile, it had to be honest and deal with all problems that would come up in discussions. Too, any parent could visit the class or talk with me if they wanted any clarification on what the class was like or doing.

The course was then presented to the board; my principal presented the class and got board acceptance. I felt I had backing for the class from my local community all the way to the elected school board. Starting the following year with a class of three sections, adding an additional section each year 'til now I teach only human relations and we are in need of additional teachers. Too, the course has developed greater interest in psychology and next year this course will be offered.

JERRY: Later we will hear from your students regarding their perceptions and reactions to their class, but would you say something now about the reactions you get from fellow faculty members and from your administration? What kind of feedback do you get from parents? LINDA: When the class was first added to the curriculum, the first reaction was oh—a sex education class, who's going to teach THAT! Once we were over that hurdle, the class is well received by most faculty members. They have a good relationship with me and the only area we may disagree on is that I want the students to *feel* and they want the students to *think*.

I have always felt that the administration has backed me. No, I have not always been able to do everything I want; I have had to make compromises, but I felt the administration had the class first in mind and were really concerned that matters work out best for it so that a positive reaction in the community was maintained. I have always checked with the administration when I felt the need to have backing or to let them know what was going on in the class. I have tried to work within the structure that is provided in my district and I have a very caring, humanistic school administration that holds student interest and learning in high regard.

Parents in the community have very positive comments to make about this class. Remember that I only have students whose parents gave permission to take the class. Many parents have said that they are much closer to their son/daughter as a result of what has happened in the class. They are glad their child has a place to go to discuss problems and to get answers to questions that at times they don't know how to deal with.

JERRY: What are some of the most exciting and rewarding things you've experienced in your classes this semester? LINDA: To me the most rewarding experience is when a student tells me that he has learned a lot from this (about himself and others) class, that he has become involved in his own learning and self-growth.

It is very rewarding to see students assume more and more responsibility for their own learning, and to see students relating with each other in a more open, trusting way. I also experience many deep and meaningful relationships with my students on a personal level.

JERRY: How much of yourself do you choose to share with your students? Do you feel comfortable in self-disclosure with your students? Do you let them know how you feel? What effect does your own transparency have upon your students? LINDA: I try to be as real a person in my class as I can. I show anger when it happens, have cried when I was sad, and laughed with my class. I have become comfortable in telling my class my own feelings, even when I am intellectualizing an answer and cannot be sure if I could emotionally do what I say I think is best. I try not to preach and only give my opinion if someone asks. I don't feel that my opinion is most important; I believe that the opinions that students are forming are much more important. The students at first are not used to a teacher showing her feelings and don't know how to deal with this fact. However, they begin to see me as an individual with feelings, to see me as a person that cares about them as individuals and wants to help them grow, and I feel that by me being real and showing feelings helps to reach this goal.

JERRY: I wonder if you care to share some personal growth experience that has been a factor in increasing your effectiveness as a teacher? How do you feel you have changed, both as a person and as a teacher, since you began teaching five years ago?

LINDA: One of the most important factors in my own growth has been the fact that I have gotten myself put together. I have answered many of my own questions as to who am I and what do I want out of life. I feel that before a teacher can deal with these same matters in classrooms, she or he must have first dealt this in her own life. How did I do this? From my own experience in groups, my own search for learning and continued GROWTH. I believe a person must never stop growing or he becomes stagnant and in a rut. DULL. My first experiened in teaching was very traditional. It's safe there—you have books, questions, study guides, and films. Put all these together and you can pretty much fill up a semester. To not always be sure of what is going to happen next, not know all the answers, can be scary at times. But the rewards to this type of risk taking are uncountable. The learning that takes place in the classroom outmeasures the learning that often takes place in the above described.

I find that as a person, I have become warmer and more loving. I have truly become a person, I am not a machine that computes but one that feels and grows, one that responds, I am alive! This is how I teach my class to be alive, to respond, to grow, to have fun—that's what life is and what learning can be.

I stay in teaching and stay being a teacher because I like kids, I like the challenge, and I want to change many things in the system I feel need to change education into a more humanistic, self-growth process, that can take place best within the system rather than destroying the system.

WHAT STUDENTS SAY ABOUT LINDA SCHNEIDER AND HER HUMAN RELATIONS
CLASS

Question: How does it feel to be a student in this class?

Student Responses

- I liked being a student in this class because I learned more about my own feelings, why I have them, and also I learned a lot about others feelings.
- Sort of weird cause I wasn't used to the freeness of it.
- It feels fine! (now) Before it was kind of scary because of all the things that had to be brought out about ourselves. The things I found out about myself was at times very frightening. But now that I know my faults and strengths, which I have learned in this class, I feel more comfortable.
- It is kind of scary because you are so much on your own. You have to make the class interesting. The students are the ones who really conduct this class. I feel pressured alot because of this responsibility. But it makes me feel good because I know I can do and learn what I want to learn and the way I want to learn it.

Question: What do you most like about this class?

- Learning about others—experiencing others' experiences and feelings towards many problems we have.
- I like the freedom that is given to the students. With this freedom you have more responsibility to learn and make something of the class. The students learn more and have more interest in what they do because they have the initiative. They do what they want to do for the most part of it.
- It's openness. We can study anything we want. We are very free to do what we feel. We aren't forced to follow a certain guideline where we have to have certain things done at certain times.

Question: Describe in your own words how you see your teacher. How you feel toward your teacher?

- My teacher is one of the most beautiful, sensitive, giving women I have ever known. I don't think of her as a teacher but as a friend who through helping me learns with me. I've become fairly close to her in the last two years. She is a good friend that I hope I never lose contact with.
- I see my teacher not as a teacher but as a real person. I look at her as a very warm person with feelings and emotions. This I rarely find in a teacher.
- The teacher is most attractive, which I think could distract the

male mind. The male in the classroom is what I am talking about. I'm not saying that attractive teachers should not teach human relations but they shouldn't look so foxy!

- I see Mrs. Schnider as a person who can open up and talk to people, and is one that doesn't put up a big front like most teachers.
- I like my teacher. I feel that she is one of the most honest teachers in the school because she sees the kids more as human beings and not as numbers like some teachers do, or as "the enemy" as some teachers do. She usually took our feelings into consideration.
- She teaches her classes in a very openly and comfortable way. Being a good friend and also a guide. She has opened up my mind and I've become more of my own person—like she is.
- Linda is very hard to describe for me, because I feel she is so many wonderful and beautiful things, all wrapped up into one package. She is patient, understand, lovable, capable, she knows what she wants and gets it but she is also human. She has taught me so many things, to have her as a teacher has been an experience.
- I feel Mrs. Sneider is a truly beautiful person. She's so understanding and always so open with everything especially sex. Too many other teachers would be afraid to do this because they have too many hang-ups about sex. Also she treats us like adults and not babies like some teachers do.

Question: How do you feel your teacher sees you as a class?

- I feel that my teacher thinks of me more as a friend than a student. I think she feels about the same way towards me as I feel towards her. She doesn't put herself on a high pedastol and think of herself as a teacher and me the student. In fact I would say that she feels as if she is a student herself because she learns with us.
- I think our teacher sees us not as a high school class but as a group of young people searching for some real truth and meaning to our lives.
- Usually she tries to react to us as people, though sometimes she gets mad and slips into the authoritarian role. I know that sometimes she was disappointed in us and frustrated at the way the class went, but I think she understood the problems people in the class had in discussing things.

Question: What are some things about this class that are different from your other classes?

- 1. The freedom of choice.
  2. They treat you as an adult in this class, they don't worry about petty rules such as tardies etc.
  3. The students conduct the class.
  4. If you wish not to do anything in the class that's your initiative.

    5. You don't learn or study from books.
    6. There are no tests or homework.
    7. It's a harder class than any other class I've had.
    8. It makes you think and learn in a different and interesting way.
    9. It gives you a chance to be yourself and express your opinions.
   10. It gives you the right to make mistakes and be able to lift your-
        self up without the threat of grades (pass–fail).

- This class is much more loosely put together. There are no tardies, seating chart, or rules about raising hands and not talking. The class operates on the consideration of the members toward each other, and usually that solved all the problems. We have almost complete freedom with the curriculum, and plan our own activities.
- People are more freer with ideas and feelings in this class and there is a more comfortable atmosphere. In other classes you have to watch what you say.
- This class has been the best thing that I have ever gotten into. I have learned more things about myself and other people, and have done more serious, hard, down-to-earth thinking this semester than I've done in the past three years of high school.
- I really enjoyed being in your class, and I felt you have showed me a lot of things—like loving, caring, being patient, understanding—all the things that matter to get along in this world with people, you helped me in my times of need and loneliness. If I knew I had noone to talk to I always felt I had you. I feel you are the greatest, most emotional and caring teacher I know. I feel you are the only teacher in this god-damn school who cares and knows *ME*. Because you took the time to find out about me you been good to me and I'll always love you for that.

AN INTERVIEW WITH RICHARD JACOBS
WORLD HISTORY TEACHER
DUARTE HIGH SCHOOL, DUARTE, CALIFORNIA

Of all of the four teachers, Richard Jacobs is probably the most radical. By appearance alone he might seem radical; yet his influence is far more subtle. As a teacher with more than ten years of experience, he is justifiably angered at what he sees as destructive features of formal education. He *does* propose an alternative. Instead of subjecting his students to a deadening version of world history, he has found creative ways of really involving his students in crucial issues that have faced mankind. He encourages them to think about the story of man, and he helps them to think about and see how history is currently being written. He continually seeks for methods of capturing the interests and stimulating thought with his students.

Richard Jacob's approach is experimental, and he grasps new ideas as the course progresses. His role is more of a director, initiator, and resource person than a lecturer. Richard has chosen to work mainly in schools with minority students. From my many visits to his class, it is obvious that the black students he teaches have real respect and affection for him. As a white teacher, Richard Jacobs has been extremely effective in demonstrating his understanding of his black and Chicano students. He recalls:

> My college preparation for teaching did not include courses concerning the minority. There weren't any. After passing the exams for a position in the L.A. City, I recall one question at the interview before being hired: "Do you object to teaching minority children?" I said "No," and was immediately placed in a school where the majority consisted of minority students. I also recall being forced to sign numerous, rather legal-looking documents declaring I was not a communist and taking several loyalty oaths, but I was never asked if I belonged to the Ku Klux Klan or the American Nazi Party before placement with those black and brown children.

Here is another illustration that there are imaginative ways of reaching our students. In spite of the fact that the course is required, and the students are compelled to attend, there are ways of discovering a format where students at least have the opportunity of getting involved.

JERRY COREY: What are the things you most want to accomplish with your class in world history this year?

RICHARD JACOBS: Well, first of all, I had to destroy the implicit intentions of the course itself. World History was really the thrice-told tale (elementary, junior high, high school) of how white Western man spread out from Europe to civilize and conquer the "natives" of the remainder of the world. It was slanted, narrow, and biased history. It reinforces the destructive forces of racism and intolerance in our society. To "teach it" to a class where minority students comprise a sizeable number is a method of cultural genocide I did not care to be a part of.

Even within the narrow channels of the traditional course, the material consisted of the usual succession of chronological events that detailed the fortunes of kings and generals whose constant adventures in wars provided many pages of maps that reflected the constantly changing boundaries in a particularly wrinkled and squeezed area of the globe called "Europe."

In a school that had known racial disturbances and lack of communication and understanding among its divided student population, I am attempting to present materials that show the richness and beauty inherent in the diversity of man. I am also attempting to present "ideas as history," contemporary issues in a direct and meaningful way, avoiding the usual gutted and vacuous summary that composes the content of the secondary school history.

JERRY: What are some unique features about your course? How does it differ from a traditional method of teaching history?
RICHARD: I abandoned the designated textbook the first day of class. Here we were, sitting together in a classroom, without the sole source of knowledge that the district and taxpayers had given us. What were we going to do? What did we want to learn? How would we learn it? We made a long list of things that interested us that included drugs, international trade, human rights, communism, Vietnam, technology and world power, world ecology, races of mankind, status of women, poverty, assassinations, civil disobedience, the world of the future, war, minorities of the world, man before history, great dissenters, atomic bombing of Japan, divided nations, generations under twenty-five, profiles of courage, etc. Now, how were we going to learn about these things?

I did not want the success of the students to be dependent on the one rather special skill—reading—that schools and classes demand as the only media through which students may escape failure. I also wanted to provide divergent as well as convergent opportunities for the students. These learning opportunities must offer some possibility of creative activity and personal interpretation. I suggested that the students choose one topic and do several things with it. The amount of effort and each emphasis in activity would be up to the student. One activity would be to create a game, complete with gameboard, tokens, cards, dice, etc. that used the topic as background for the game. Another approach was to write a short story with the characters involved in a story line that used the topic selected; another activity involved creating a collage that portrayed the topic; yet another method was to contact directly an agency or organization in the greater metropolitan area that was involved in the topic and obtain information. The student was also to invite a speaker from that agency to come to the class and talk about the subject. The final project was to research the subject in the traditional academic method and write a paper.

This idea of bringing into the classroom the rich resources of the greater community resulted in a very exciting program that soon involved many students outside my classroom. In the early days of the semester we were discussing the origin of man. Several students were confused and distressed that the theory of evolution did not jive with the Christian fundamentalist view they had received from home and church. I invited two ministers from the community and two science teachers on the staff to attend an all-day seminar on "The Origin of Man" in my classroom. I also invited teachers to bring their classes in to hear the speakers and allowed interested students, with the permission of their teachers, to attend. The room was full each period, and despite the fact that the structure tended to defeat the purpose (bells ringing, teacher complaints of unfair competition, administration concern regarding the movement and mobility of students, etc.), the seminars engaged the students in a stimulating discussion that drew sharp exchanges between the differing participants. The next seminar came out of a discussion regarding ancient Egypt and the burial of the Pharoahs in the pyramids. The importance of death in ancient Egypt was compared with the significance of death in present American society. "The Significance of Death in American Society" seminar had a distinguished panel of people that included a nationally renowned scientist from the City of Hope, a psychologist who was a professor at the local college, two ministers, and a school psychologist from the district office.

Students also arranged seminars and guest speakers that included members of the Sierra Club; representatives of the Women's Liberation movement attempted to explain this new frontier of freedom to a jammed room of students; the warrior chief of the Sioux Nation told with great dignity the suffering and plight of the American Indian; the dread consequences of drug abuse were conveyed by a social worker, a nurse at a drug clinic, a deputy sheriff, and an ex-addict. I received the ire of a city councilman when, in a seminar discussing the newly-enfranchised eighteen-year-old voter, I had the candidate of the Socialist Workers Party for President of the United States along with representatives of other political groups discuss this topic. Over fifty people visited my classes during this one semester. Individuals from the United Nations Association talked about world hunger. A representative from the American Friends exchanged viewpoints with a member of the military concerning the necessity and justification of war.

JERRY: Would you give us some examples of the kinds of issues you deal with in your world history class? What's the course content like?
RICHARD: Aside from the seminars I have previously discussed, we have explored many issues that are of concern to the students. In some of my classes we set up a series of debates between teams of students taking pro and con positions on issues such as the legalization of pot, abortion, the selective service, the space program, and police behavior. It was the responsibility of each team to prepare their case through research. They were also urged to call expert witnesses. A group of students judged the procedings and awarded points based on the ability of students to document their statements and prepare sound positions. The expert witnesses were cross-examined in a spirited fashion. In the abortion debate, for example, a Catholic priest spoke against the subject in question; a counselor from a free clinic was the witness for the affirmative position. There were occasionally tense moments as when representatives of Chicano Barrio Self-Defense Committee confronted a deputy sheriff in an angry dialogue that reflected the depth of feeling and distance of thinking in this matter. I feel that the importance and significance of these seminars and debates were not simply in the information that was dispensed but more importantly in the fact they could view, perhaps for the first time in their lives, adults discussing, with vigor and passion, the ideas, concepts, and issues that confront and divide our society. What a contrast between this and the picked-over bones that lay buried in the drab concensus of a textbook!

I was also able to obtain paperback series dealing with such topics as authority, poverty, race, drugs, world religions, violence, revolutions, etc.

JERRY: What do you think the present school system does to the learner—from elementary school through high school? What are you attempting to do about this in your classroom?

RICHARD: I have found that the present school system does different things to different learners. If the learner can "match up" in several ways that require certain values, background, and experiences, he has a fighting chance. It also does some things to all its learners; the school system places prime value on the custodial possession of the student's physical self in a designated place in an immobile state for a certain number of hours per day. The teacher too often places prime value on the transfer of stale and "cold" information through the media of his voice to the student. Students will no longer sit still for this type of exchange to take place. They have better ways of learning information, at least more efficient ways: the mass media, friends, direct experience. Today's students are no longer preparing for life; they are living it. They have been trained and encouraged to surrender the initiative and responsibility for their own learning experiences. By the time they reach the secondary school, students have lost faith in the possibility that the classroom could be a site for something of significance to happen to them. More often they know of it as a place of frustration and failure. Charles Silberman in *Crisis in the Classroom* describes the classrooms as joyless and sterile places.

Perhaps this would be the best place to describe my classroom. It is very difficult to portray and project this classroom without having you enclosed within it. The walls are painted from floor to ceilings with paintings, images, grafitti, caligraphy, and symbols that reflect the youth that live there. This is a multi-racial student body and "black is beautiful" is stretched across one wall and "white is wonderful" is on another. "Viva La Raza" and "Red is Right" (Indian-type red) can also be seen in this vibrant room. The students have also painted the light fixtures that hang from the ceiling. The ceiling itself is covered with stapled boards that contain collages, abstract designs, and bright splashes of color. The windows are covered with curtains that have been covered with tie-dye and batik techniques. Students have also brought in old, upholstered furniture and carpets. The room reflects the vitality and excitement of its inhabitants. It is their room. They know it.

JERRY: Perhaps you would care to comment on the ways you are seen by fellow teachers. What kinds of reactions to your program do you receive from parents?

RICHARD: I must admit to having certain feelings about this that make an attempt at objectivity difficult. It seems too many teachers unfortunately reach a point of frustration where they adopt a cops-and-robbers or cowboys-and-Indians approach to teaching. If they observe a break in the ranks of teacher soldiery from a teacher who identifies himself too closely with the students, this traitor to his class and caste is not forgiven easily. If these students happen to be black or brown, the implications are often viewed as a threat by many teachers. I have been in teaching situations where, at a time of tension or trouble, I was informed that "one of my students" started the trouble. The student, of course, was not on my class roll but was black or brown.

Teachers are the successful products of the system they re-enter as teachers. There is a great tendency to perpetuate that system and when assessing difficulties place the overwhelming responsibility for any malfunction in the system on the students. A teacher who attempts to bring about changes in some basic manner and questions some of the basic premises inherent in the present structure is bound to become the source of some discomfort. I must confess I have been surprised and dismayed by the intensity of the reaction at times. I would also say that things have changed in the last few years. Events in society and the active awareness of minority groups have forced some changes. The literature regarding education today has caught up with me and I find it very supportive; increasing numbers of teachers are being exposed to Holt, Neill, Silberman, Kohl, Rogers, Leonard, etc.

JERRY: What do you get from being a teacher? Why do you remain in the profession? What personal needs are met through your work?
RICHARD: After eleven years in education, I still think being present at the celebration of a new idea when first perceived by a student to be of great value and satisfaction to me. I am also fortunate not to be a materialist by preference so that the necessity of giving up those kinds of desires upon entering teaching was made less difficult. I also think that generally I prefer the company of young people to that of adults. It is not because I view them as less threatening but because the "process of becoming" is more visible, if indeed it is even present, in most adults.

I find students a very dependable source of love and affection. This continuing source, particularly at the times when my personal life is lacking in this area, has been of great comfort to me. It also provides an honest feedback of how others perceive me. This, of course, only happens when you encourage open and honest behavior. I do. I also take advantage of being able to act out my feelings and to act upon ideas, knowing that I am certain of some kind of reaction from others.

WHAT STUDENTS SAY ABOUT RICHARD JACOBS AND HIS HISTORY CLASS

Question: How does it feel to be a student in this class?

Student Responses

- I feel very comfortable in this class, I think I have learned plenty in this class about today.
- To be a student in this class you go through an experience you'll never forget. Because the teacher runs the class different from any other teacher, at Duarte High School. I feel I learn more from Jacobs than any other teacher.
- not to good because iam not sopos to be I her because I am in the 11 grade and this is a 10 grade class
- It feels far-out to Be a Student in Jake's class.
- I'm a Black Student and its very hard to feel like a person in D. H. S. But thru one class and thats Mr. Jacobs. He's a very wonderful person.
- I really like being in this class. If I didn't have this class, I don't think I would come to school. I dislike school but when I come in here I can go on the rest of the day.

Question: What do you like most about this class?

- The freedom and relaxed atmosphere. Because when the pressure is off you learn better.
- I like the freedom to explore more than just what is in history books. I like to be able to investigate the areas I am interested in.
- (1) The seminars (2) Freedom to cut when you don't feel you can make it (3) Projects

Question: What are some of the most exciting and rewarding things you've done in the class so far?

- I think the seminars were really rewarding because they really made me think about the world around me.
- I enjoyed the seminars especially and guest speakers.
- I did a report of poverty. It was very rewarding because it made me see what I wanted to do when I get out of school.

Question: Please use the rest of the space to write any comments you have about the class, the teacher, or any observations you care to make.

- I like Mr. Jacobs way of teaching very most. I remember last year I hated history and all of the lies. I even did not like white people because they always won.
- This is the best class I've ever taken. I can learn what I want and don't have to learn about the same junk I've learned about for 8 years.

- He's an outstanding teacher friend and fellow human being.
- This class awful damn good I love it

The following two articles were published in the school newspaper and were included because they show how students feel toward Richard Jacobs and his work at the school.

He tries. The man REALLY tries. In a school year that has been typically devoid of intellectual stimulation, Richard Jacobs has come through. All year he has sponsored seminar discussions that have packed his vibrant classroom with people. Subjects have ranged from the American Indian to death and the theory of evolution. And, last week, he invited representatives of three political parties and one political organization to speak on the eighteen-year-old vote.

This seminar became a center of controversy in the City of Duarte. A councilman objected strongly and vocally to the appearance of Linda Jenness, Socialist Workers Party candidate for President. The councilman released a news statement attacking Jacobs and the school for allowing such a thing to happen. However, true to Mr. Jacob's form, Ms. Jenness appeared.

The seminar was interesting, even though it seemed to me that the Democratic and Republican representatives were giving us a bunch of B.S. and even though they seemed to beat around the bush. People in attendance were exposed to the SWP philosophy, and were probably totally frustrated, as I was, by the Democratic and Republican "answers." The main purpose of the seminar was achieved, however: long after the speakers had left, students were still discussing what they had said.

The students and faculty of this school really owe Mr. Jacobs a thank-you for providing learning experiences outside the traditional structured classroom atmosphere. It's a big step in the right direction.

● ● ●

During the past few months Duarte High's Mr. Dick Jacobs has been sponsering a series of discussion groups.

Mr. Jacobs assigned the program as part of a long-term assignment to his Modern World History classes. He felt the students should search out the information themselves. Originally they were supposed to tape an interview with a speaker; however, due to the unavailability of the tape-recorder a better idea evolved. If a recording couldn't be brought back, why not the speaker?

Guests from many important organizations and agencies were provided and a wide variety of topics were discussed. The first of these was "The Origin of Man." Mr. Frank and Dr. Venerable from Duarte High's faculty expressed the scientific viewpoint. The religious opinion was given by Rev. Huffy and Rev. Vamboening.

"*The Significance of Death in Our American Society*," the second of these seminars, also gave a religious and scientific aspect. Speakers included Dr. Roberts, a scientist from the City of Hope; Dr. Corey, a professor and psychologist at Cal Poly, Rev. Ray and Dr. Holly from the district.

These discussions covered current and controversial subjects. "World Hunger" was discussed by representatives from the United Nations Association. The Women's Liberation Movement was also covered with a speaker from the Women's Center in Los Angeles. Mr. Owens and Mr. Johnson, teachers from Duarte High, spoke on "Black Pride."

The most recent seminar, "Questions and Problems of Pollution in Our Ecology" had Mr. Hutton, a representative from the Sierra Club; Mr. John Wyatt, from General Motors; Clark Dawson from the United Ecology Association; and Mr. Music of Southern California Edison Company. In the near future drugs will be the topic of discussion.

When asked the reason for these seminars, Mr. Jacobs replied with, "I felt a commitment that high schools should enrich their courses by taking advantage of the Los Angeles cultural resources. I'm pleased with the interested student's response and perhaps their intellectual curiosity has been grossly underestimated."

Mr. Jacobs hopes these seminars will become a regular part of the school with the total student body involved, and discussions held once or twice a month.

SUMMARY: SOME THREADS IN COMMON

It is obvious that all four of these teachers have something in common: in a very real sense they are lovers. They love their work; their love for their students as persons comes through in their writing; and the love they receive from the students is apparent. While each of these teachers expresses love for students, none of them are caught in the trap of needing to love all students, nor do they feel a need to love them equally. These four teachers can *be* their feelings, and they can express these feelings in their classrooms. The ability to respect, trust, and appreciate young people is also apparent in their writings. These teachers are earning the genuine respect and love from their students by what they are becoming as persons—loving, caring, honest teachers.

Another common denominator of these teachers is that they view their students as potentially mature persons, who have a will to learn and who will generally function well when they are trusted. They do not share the pessimistic view of the depraved nature of man that so many teachers seem to hold. Because they expect students to respond affirmatively, the students usually learn how to cope with freedom and responsibility.

Rather than viewing the teacher's role as a conveyor of information, these teachers see their function as helper, facilitator, resource person, consultant, behind-the-scene manager, and counselor. They work *with* students, and they are relinquishing their role as a "stand up in front of class and tell 'em and then test 'em."

Each of these teachers assumes the role of learner. Their students frequently commented that the line between teacher and student is sometimes fuzzy and that their teachers are open to new learning from students. And these teachers are crucially concerned with the lives of the students they taught. Each of them exhibits a real effort to gear his course to the outside lives of the young people; each attempts to relate the course to their concerns. In doing this, these teachers move away from textbooks and tests and toward more student input and initiative.

8

The Challenge of
Revolutionizing our Schools

I want to share with you an experience of working as a consultant with five public high school teachers in their effort to establish a "school within a school" or, as they called it, a "New School."

One teacher, disillusioned by the restrictions and limitations of traditional education, requested my support in assisting a team of five teachers to develop and implement a more humanistic approach toward teaching and learning. This group had already devoted weeks of their free time in planning for the establishment of a "New School" within their school. At faculty meetings they continually addressed themselves to essential matters, and raised questions for faculty discussion such as: Why is there such apathy and indifference on the part of our student body? Why are so many failing in our courses? What do the high truancy and drop-out rates tell us? Are the violence, gang fighting, destruction of property, and general rebellion clues that we are failing to provide a meaningful education for our students? What can we do within our classes to provide maximum freedom for their own learning? How can we lessen student hostility and create a climate where students and teachers together can engage in learning activities that have personal relevance?

Unfortunately, these questions raised by this small group of "rebels" fell on deaf ears. As a group, the faculty countered with such comments as:

- "Let's get down to practical matters. What are we going to do about students who come late to our classes? What about those who cut classes? Let's set down more rigid rules so they know we mean business!"
- "And what about the students who park in our faculty lot? Let's have someone posted to catch the culprits!"
- "We ought to clamp down on the kids who aren't doing their homework. Maybe we can have a policy on this!"
- "The student dress is outrageous! Girls with those short skirts who are bordering on immodesty are a distraction to learning. Let's measure their skirt length to see if it's appropriate. And we need to set definite limits for hair on boys. I suggest no beards surely. Sideburns, if we must allow them, ought not to be any lower than the ear lobe. And let's *insist* on appropriate hair cuts."

165

And so the tenor of the meetings went—a preoccupation with control of the unruly mob that could revolt at any time unless severe and oppressive measures were taken to keep them under control. The concerns of these five faculty members, who were all new teachers on this staff, were met with silence at best and with hostile indignation by many. "What are you guys trying to do, anyway? Whose side are you on? Ours or theirs?"

This lonely group of five did not despair when they were confronted with faculty indifference and hostility—the first barrier to constructive change along humanistic lines. Instead, they discussed their ideas of forming a school within a school with their principal. He responded favorably, encouraged them to proceed, and informed them he would support their efforts, but that he wanted the project to be their project, not his.

The New School pioneering group continued the necessary groundwork, which included:

1. Conducting a survey to determine the degree to which the school was effectively meeting the needs of the student body.
2. Doing research on students who entered a college or university after graduation. (They found less than five graduates of the high school entered the University of California; less than five of the graduates entered the state college system; and less than one half of the graduates went on to any form of higher education. And this was a "College Preparatory" school with approximately 2000 students!)
3. Surveying student attitudes. They found widespread evidence of apathy, indifference, and hostility. Only a small percentage of students were involved in extracurricular activities. Student government was ineffective, with only a select few participating. There was much evidence of tension and misunderstanding among races.
4. Studying faculty turnover rates. One-third of the faculty were new that year. The administrative and counseling staff had even a higher turnover rate.
5. Formulating definite objectives, drawing up a detailed proposal for the New School, working on course outlines, with new approaches to be used, all with the input of student groups. They sampled student opinion to assess which changes were most needed.
6. Stating specific behaviorial objectives and listing specific types of objective measures to assess the degree of effectiveness of this New School approach.

7. Agreeing to take thirty-five students each (their normal student load), which would mean that the student body of the New School would consist of 175 students.
8. Establishing selection procedures and criteria.
9. Outlining the organizational structure of the New School.
10. Forming a faculty advisory group from members of this school and others within the district.
11. Contacting all the major colleges and universities in the surrounding area to recruit free consultation services, use of graduate students in education, etc. They did enlist this help; and letters of support, promising free assistance, were sent to the Board of Education by various colleges.
12. *Not* requesting any additional funding by the district. They were wise enough to know that seeking additional funds from a district which already was experiencing financial pains would mean the sudden death of their project. Instead, they contacted community agencies, and a nonprofit cooperation was to be formed for the purpose of raising the budget from private sources. Foundations, government agencies, and industries interested in educational innovation were asked to assist in funding the project and helping in other ways. This group was successful in soliciting help from these groups.
13. Contacting both the Superintendent and the Assistant Superintendent and giving a presentation. These top-level administrators were cautiously supportive, but emphasized that the entire high school faculty should be sympathetic to this pilot program to insure its effectiveness.
14. Giving a presentation to the school board, and informing parents of the plans for a school within a school on an experimental pilot-program basis.

It should be clear by now that the teachers spent many extra hours of their energy to establish this program. They worked late into evening hours and on their week-ends as well. No one could legitimately accuse them of ignoring the necessary groundwork to get their project into operation. At this point, I would like to present more detail concerning the proposal for the New School.

THE GOAL

The New School would be structured to give the students maximum responsibility for their own education. The present school structure was viewed as inflexible, unresponsive to students' needs, and unlikely to solve the existing problems on the campus. The main goals of the New School were to help students build more positive self-concepts; to provide a climate where the student could develop attitudes and values which were more open, tolerant, flexible, and accepting; to encourage a greater degree of creativity and diversity; and to provide a place where the student could initiate, define, and evaluate his own learning projects. Further goals were to encourage student involvement in the school and community and greater student awareness of the pressing problems in contemporary society and the world, as well as study of possible solutions to our major local, state, and international problems.

SELECTION PROCEDURE AND CRITERIA

All students would be informed of the formation of the New School. Letters were to be sent to parents of all freshman and sophomore students inviting them to make further inquiries about the program. The selection criteria were:

1. Students must learn to read and write.
2. Students must agree to become participating members of the New School.
3. The student body should be a heterogeneous group, with respect to ability, sex, and race.
4. Students' parents are to agree to allow their student to participate fully in the New School program.

ORGANIZATION OF THE NEW SCHOOL

The school would operate on a pass–fail basis. The schedule of the school would be informal and run without bells. A weekly schedule would be prepared for each student, and individuals were to be responsible to be present as required. There are the following kinds of activities that would be undertaken in the New School:

1. *Seminars:* While seminars would vary in size according to topic and purpose, they would be used to discuss speakers, field trips, readings, and general class discussions. College students (teacher trainees) were to be used as seminar leaders. Seminar questions might include: What do I value? Who are my heroes? What is thinking? Can I separate fact from fiction? Does my culture reward honesty?

2. *Directed Study:* In an area of directed study, the staff would attempt to help students outline areas for pursuit, tailored to the needs of the individual student. The traditional subjects would not be covered in fifty-minute categorized periods; rather they would be covered with emphasis on the individual student's ability to relate the subject matter to his own self and his own situation.

3. *Tutoring:* Peer group members, college students, community volunteers, and staff were to be available to work directly with students on a one-to-one basis until basic skills had been achieved.

4. *Presentation:* Students, faculty, and special guest speakers from colleges and the community were part of the design and were to make presentations in lecture or panel form.

5. *Experimental Studies:* Here is the area where emphasis would be placed on the creative approach of the individual or group to their own interest. It was envisioned that this area was where the New School could exercise the most flexibility and mobility in the pursuit of these interests. Some examples could include:

   (a) Walking tours of the city and community to discover its problems and potentials.

   (b) Day trips to schools, factories, hospitals, and other public institutions.

   (c) Extended trips to the mountains, desert, and sea to study ecology or natural environment.

   (d) Extended trips studying a divergent culture, such as Chinatown, a ghetto, or a barrio setting, to acquire insights into divergent patterns of culture.

   (e) An exchange between families of students from divergent cultural backgrounds.

   (f) Original plays, films, and musical events produced by students.

   (g) Simulation games used to study such subjects as the free enterprise system, open housing, and other life-like situations.

   (h) Noncompetitive physical activities such as dance, classical, folk, and contemporary; and team sports for personal enrichment, hiking, swimming, horseback riding, archery, etc.

   (i) Creative development through various art activities.

   (j) Observation of government in operation and participation in activities of community and civic groups; research on issues of local and national importance.

6. *Independent Study:* Each student in the New School was to be encouraged to undertake the study of some special interest subject and be given guidance by a staff member in the pursuit of this chosen subject. College, industry, and community people were to be utilized to provide guidance for students. Examples of subjects of independent study projects might include computer programming, landscape gardening, foreign language, science, math, metal

or woodworking, auto mechanics, food preparation, horse training, navigation, forestry, and mythology.

EVALUATION IN THE NEW SCHOOL

Evaluation procedures, both subjective and objective, were developed to assess the effectiveness of this approach. Tests would be administered at the beginning of the school year, and posttesting would be
conducted at the end of the year for the purposes of evaluation and
comparison with the regular school. Specific criteria and measuring
devices were a part of the proposal.

THE OUTCOMES OF THIS PROJECT

Sadly enough the New School never got off the ground. It was
grounded before it could be put into the initial stage of operation. One
wonders why such a potentially exciting model for reformation of a
dead high school program was not given a chance.

As mentioned, this project had the encouragement of the principal,
and tentative approval was given by the superintendent of the district.
What happened to sabotage the New School idea? Several faculty
members had strong feelings that such a program, even of an experimental, pilot nature, would destroy the structure of the school, and
that students might suffer permanent injury. A small cadre of these
anti-New School militants marched to the school board and protested
loudly. These teachers were mainly part of the established "old guard"
who had served the school for decades.

What are the barriers to change? Why is any innovation perceived
as a threat? And why do some teachers invest so much energy in
thwarting any novel ideas of a group who really want to effect constructive change? Here we have five dedicated teachers who had gone
beyond the stage of endlessly complaining about the ills of the system
and had worked diligently at presenting a viable alternative to a deadening education. What was their fate? They were told to wait for a
few years, put more work on the proposal in the meantime, and try
again later.

One key barrier to any education change is that any substantial
departure from the known is almost always perceived as threatening
by teachers who are locked into the traditional system. Such teachers
have invested much of themselves to preserve the status quo; any novel
forms of education threaten this rigid framework. Out of their fear

of experimenting with new approaches themselves, they find fault with any potential rebel who might disturb their predictable and safe systems. Because of their own insecurity, they cannot tolerate any potentially successful endeavor by others. Imagine the effects upon the old guard if the New School were put into full operation and it succeeded. What a contrast! The old guard's traditional program would pale by comparison, and those who defended the status quo might be forced to change.

To give you a fuller picture of the nature of this resistance, I want to share some criticisms made by one of the faculty members who led the crusade for the demolition of the New School. The comments are taken from a report he wrote entitled *Critique of the "New School" Concept.*

In response to the statement that the New School would be structured to give the students maximum responsibility for their own education, this protesting faculty member leveled the following criticism: "Where do students get the experience to make this kind of decision with discretion? Experienced, responsible administrators and educators *cannot* be replaced in this decision by inexperienced students or parents who are unfamiliar with the field of education."

As was mentioned in the New School proposal, competition of student against student would be deemphasized or, ideally, discarded. The criticism of this change was:

> Competition and challenge are rudimentary to the American way of life. It is better to have tried and failed than not to have tried at all. Awareness of self is fine, but that self must still compete and run the risk of failing. The "New School" would have *pass or fail grades* and *no bell schedules*—thus eliminating competition and challenge from the curriculum.

Another criticism: "Accusation has been made that the present structure fails the student in his search for personal relevance, but there is *no* evidence that a more liberal structure will work any better. The "New School" will be gambling with the lives of 175 students."

The faculty member who so vehemently opposed this experimental program deeply felt that students need stricter discipline from authorities, and he viewed the proposed freedom to be granted students as an invitation to unbridled chaos and student rebellion. Listen to his words:

> You don't get anything in society without work and discipline. Payton Jordan, track coach at Stanford University said, . . . "There are two kinds of discipline. One is imposed . . . for the young and the

immature; you owe it to them to help them establish their personal habits, to give them guidelines for sensible and productive character. The other discipline is that which is self-imposed for the responsible individual or adult. Failure for self-imposed discipline on the part of students is evident today by riots, anarchy, and revolution on college and high school campuses." Yet the "New School" advocates presuppose that students can self-discipline themselves in the face of no grades and no bell schedule and optimum opportunity to educate themselves. The spirit of this campus cries for discipline. And *they* would have students come and go as they wish!

The concluding words of this faculty protestor poignantly sum up the way he views students—as "inmates" to be controlled by the guards (teachers).

The procedures and methods contrived in the "New School" as being innovative are, in fact, in effect now in the regular structure of our high school. Only chaos, enmity, and division can result by the institution of a very liberal system within the heart of the structure of our high school. At any given period, the casual observer can witness students sitting idly on the campus or playing cards during class time. Is there better reason for *not* allowing a more liberal system on the campus? In the words of Payton Jordan, track coach at Stanford, "Democracy isn't very efficient—especially when you are dealing with two segments of society—those who are educated and knowledgeable and those who are still formulating character. Obviously the young and immature need guidelines and they need discipline from their parents and educators if education is to be orderly and meaningful." You don't let the inmates run the institution, do you? Then we don't let the kids run the school.

The remarks made by the faculty member who initiated the protest against the "New School" might be hilarious if they were not so tragic. The tragedy is that this teacher's view of students and what school ought to be are not atypical. I feel quite certain that people like him would have a sizeable fan club who would rally their full support for doing their duty and disciplining unruly students, which is what happened in this case.

Consider the following letter that was written to one of the teachers who was involved in the New School proposal. This letter was written by one of his fellow teachers who substituted for him one day. It is a further example of the authoritarian teacher who has as his first concern control of the masses. This letter is authentic.

In the art classes I had the students continue with their projects—and in the history classes I attempted to discuss with them the various aspects of American History, starting with Columbus—but it was a rather hopeless cause. In period 2 they would listen to some extent, but in period 5 only the two tables closest to the desk paid any attention while most everyone else engaged in gabbing, laughter, foolishness, and shenanigans. Roger jumped out the window and I sent him to the Vice Principal. Carl beat the table top in kettle-drum fashion and I sent him to Social Adjustment. In period 6 things went well until clean-up time when two of the Negro boys closest to the window spent the entire ten minutes chasing each other, and tossing wet sponges at each other—*even* during the flag salute! In period 1 Joey and Michael accused Emily and other girls at the table of having cut the brush bristles off. The girls denied it and accused the boys. At clean-up time there was a lot of noise and commotion and madness, with things flying through the air and yelling, etc. The bright spot in period 1 was Leslie and Herman who deserve orchids for being helpful. Larry, Steven, Charles, Walter, and James spent much time in the back room, saying you wanted it cleaned. I hope they left things in shape. I'm sorry I can't make a more cheerful report."

Signed,

Mr. Smith, Substitute

To some of you this letter may appear to be an exaggeration. When I accuse teachers of being insecure people who gain security by ruling in an authoritarian fashion, most teachers I have worked with through inservice programs respond with hostility and defensively assure me that only a very few fit this picture. They coldly tell me that I am unfair in upbraiding them, and that all the teachers they know *love* children and are warm and loving teachers!

Without attempting to guess the percentage of teachers who, like that substitute, are basically rigid, my experience in conducting seminars and workshops tells me that far too many are bland, dull, unexciting, unadventuresome souls, who prefer security to change. This kind of teacher is not the kind that will cause earth-shaking innovations.

The difficulty in initiating any change then is primarily to be found within the insecure, rigid, defensive teachers committed to maintaining old ways and squelching newer forms that threaten the calm order of things. The teacher himself, as a person, is the prime factor as an agent of change.

In general, I see teachers as timid, frightened of anything new, slow to change, unwilling to risk, and downright hostile and oppressive to those who threaten their peaceful existences. How, then, do we change this? How can we begin to innovate? What does it take? Sometimes in despair I almost lose any hope of some of these old guard teachers ever changing, particularly since the old guard includes young teachers with rigid ideas. My hope is that we can educate the newer teachers *as persons.* In teacher education we urgently need to devote time to assisting future teachers to develop as self-actualizing beings; we need not be so exclusively preoccupied with training new teachers with content of their subject and methods.

In his newly revised book, *The Transparent Self* (62), Sidney Jourard speaks on an education for a new society. He urges teachers to disclose their views on politics, ethics, religion, metaphysics, and family life, so that students can experience a variety of viewpoints on life. Jourard calls for those in the teaching profession to continue to grow as whole persons, rather than solely in mastery of their subject specialty. He remarks, "How splendid if teachers went not to summer school to add yet another graduate credit to their credentials, but to a 'growth center' for the awakening of more of their human potentialities" (62, p. 118).

Frankly, I see very little hope of any *real* reformation in our schools unless classroom teachers open themselves to the dire necessity for change. If they are satisfied with the authoritarian structure characterized by the master–slave relationship, why should any change come about? I am in favor of much more discriminating selection procedures to screen out candidates who cling to anti-life attitudes and who view children and youth as malleable objects to be molded arbitrarily according to their grand design. I am very much in favor of offering encounter group experiences for those who are involved in teacher preparation. The focus should not be upon sickness, but rather on providing a nonthreatening place where teacher candidates can work on their personal growth, examine their motivations for wanting to become teachers, develop and test a philosophy of education and life, and learn to relate to other persons on an I–Thou level.

So much depends on what we want our future teachers to become, and how we view their role. If we desire to produce teachers only (dispensers of information), then we will find no urgency in revamping our teacher education programs. If, on the other hand, we want persons with humanistic values who can be human instruments in the growth of young persons, then we need to do more than simply *train* teachers. In *The Transparent Self,* Jourard issues a challenge to those in "teachers colleges."

> If "teachers colleges" do not teach, but only train, and if we want and need more teachers than trainers, then it would be appropriate to invite members of the profession *to get on with their growth* so that they can encourage, not block, the growth of coming generations who will be living in and inventing the new society (62, p. 118).

What is urgently needed in education today is a recognition of the place of human relations in the classroom. The answer to our crisis in education is not to be found by constructing more elaborate buildings, but by focusing our attention on ways of encouraging and permitting the human side of the learning process. The core of the better teacher is the interpersonal relationship—between students and students, teacher and teacher, and teacher and student. In speaking of the way to resolve the problems of modern education, Carl Rogers says in *Freedom to Learn:*

> I'm sorry I can't be coolly scientific about this. The issue is too urgent. I can only be passionate in my statement that people count, that interpersonal relationships *are* important, that we could learn much more, and that unless we give strong positive attention to the human interpersonal side of our educational dilemma, our civilization is on its way down the drain. Better courses, better curricula, better courage, better teaching machines will never resolve our dilemma in a basic way. Only persons, acting as persons in their relationships with their students, can ever begin to make a dent on the most urgent problem of modern education (31, p. 125).

Teachers must learn that they *can* make a significant difference in the lives of the students they teach. They can become *therapeutic persons* without practicing psychotherapy in their classrooms. By remaining open to their own needs and by being sensitive to their own growth as persons, they can become positive influences, and agents of change. Students would then able to enhance their own being through the relationship with their human teachers and to grow through open encounter with other students. This is therapeutic (growth-inspiring) in its most real sense.

In this book *Learning to Feel–Feeling to Learn,* Hal Lyon urges educators to take the risks necessary to become persons who are concerned with developing both the intellect and the emotions of the learner. In doing so, Lyon is not suggesting that teachers should practice therapy in their classrooms. "Clearly the classroom is not the place to dig deeply into an individual's past. Educators, however, have been too shy in dealing with 'here-and-now' feelings which invariably foment between students, and between students and teachers" (28, p. 80). Lyon encourages teachers to become aware of the attitudes that restrict the growth of both the teachers and the learner. He indicates:

> What I am advocating is that they have the courage to push forward —and push hard—against the boundaries that are keeping them confined purely within the cognitive realm. They must widen their

sphere of influence to include the affective domain as well. Only by stepping out and taking inherent risks—risks which are present in all meaningful encounters—will progress be made (28, p. 81).

Herbert Kohl is an example of an educator who struggled toward honesty, self-disclosure, and authenticity in a school which was essentially authoritarian. He taught in a hostile environment; and he learned quickly that the principal was at the top, the students were at the bottom, and his job was to maintain order and control. What Kohl achieved with the students in his ghetto school lends testimony to the effects of being real, struggling to find one's own way honestly, and touching deeply the total lives of children. I recommend two books Kohl has written: *36 Children* (46) and *The Open Classroom* (45). These books have value not because they give the reader a step-by-step procedure to use, but because they can stimulate teachers to break free from established roles and find their own distinctive styles of being that fit their unique personalities. In *The Open Classroom*, Kohl suggests that we *can* become the teacher and person we never knew we could be. In his words*:

> Our schools are crazy. They do not serve the interest of adults, and they do not serve the interests of young people. They teach "objective" knowledge and its corollary, obedience to authority. They teach equality and democracy while castrating students and controlling teachers. Most of all, they teach people to be silent about what they think and feel, and worst of all, they teach people to pretend that they are saying what they think they feel. To try to break away from stupid schooling is no easy matter for teacher or student. It is a lonely and long fight to escape from believing that one needs to do what people say one should do and that one ought to be the person one is expected to be. Yet to make such an escape is a step toward beginning again and becoming the teachers we never knew we could be (45, p. 116).

CONCLUDING REMARKS

The challenge is clear. We, as educators, have the power within our very beings to revolutionize the classroom and change our classrooms from places where things interact with other things. We *can* change our classrooms from oppressive, sterile, deadening, and coer-

---

* Reprinted with permission from *The New York Review of Books.* Copyright © 1969 Herbert Kohl.

cive places where teachers play games with students and students respond by playing games to win against the teacher. If we wait passively for the public to change, or our administrators to change, then I fear for the prospects of any reformation. A beginning for us is to *feel* fully the frustration of how limiting traditional education is—for both educators and students. Once we are angry enough, and frustrated enough with the gap between what is and what could be, then real reformation is possible. We need to muster the courage to dare to be different. And we must be prepared for a lonely existence at times. The joy to be experienced in launching daring experimental ways might be well worth the price of our anxiety and loneliness. The challenge is there for us to be more than we now are—and we can choose to ignore this challenge or accept it fully. I sincerely hope that even a few educators in each school accept the challenge. To do so could well mean a complete reformation of education as we now know it.

9

Where to Go from Here

I WOULD BE AN OUTSTANDING TEACHER
IF ONLY IT WEREN'T FOR. . . .

- My authoritarian principal who is rigid and opposed to change.
- My students who insist upon a traditional classroom.
- The teacher next door who can't stand change.
- The parents who would never allow me to change.
- The Board who hands down edicts.
- My wife who nags me so that I am irritable at school.
- My husband who doesn't show me affection.
- My kids who are unruly and going through a stage of rebellion.
- The State tests.
- The teacher who gets my kids next year and expects them to know what I was supposed to teach.
- Compulsory education.
- My large classes.
- The behavior-problem kids who disrupt my class.
- My unmotivated students.
- The fact that my course is required instead of elective.
- My financial worries that bug me.
- The lack of modern textbooks.
- The behavioral objectives that I am expected to meet.
- The fact that I don't have tenure.

This list of "if only it weren't for" could be extended. The point I want to make is that we can eternally create reasons outside of ourselves to justify why we aren't the great teachers we could be. But this leaves us powerless, with little chance of becoming better teachers. There are external limitations and factors which do work against our becoming more effective teachers, but in spite of these external demands and restrictions there is a large degree of freedom within the system that most of us do not fully utilize. There are many ways of creating a more open, free, exciting climate in our classrooms where learning can be more rewarding for both the students and the teacher.

In this concluding section, a list of specific recommendations will be given. Some of these suggestions are practical, some very impractical and idealistic, some realistic. Most of these ideas relate to ways you can experiment with changing your own classroom, but some relate to things you might attempt for your own personal growth. My intention is to encourage you to add specific recommendations to this list of things you now *can* do (or would like to do) and to use some of these suggestions as a point of departure. Select any of these ideas that seem to have meaning to you and experiment. I recommend that you try some even though you may think they are silly.

1. Devote at least ten minutes each day for "alone time," where you can ask youself some essential questions of where you are going.
2. Ask yourself: What do I *most* want to accomplish as a teacher? If I accomplish nothing else, what is it that I most want to happen in my class? What are these goals important? Actually write down the answers.
3. Make a list of all of the things you do in your classroom that you feel are nonessential and that you would like to dispense with. Begin to figure out why you perform activities that seem unimportant.
4. Keep an ongoing journal—even if you make a few observations daily for only a few minutes—that describes your reactions, observations, and feelings in your daily work as a teacher.
5. Tape-record some of your classes. How much talking do you do? Do you like what you hear? What changes would you like to make?
6. Visit other schools, particularly schools that are attempting something new.
7. Come into class for *one* day (or more if you can tolerate it) without any lesson plans and just talk with the students about whatever they would like to discuss, whether it is related to your subject or not.
8. Exchange classes with a fellow teacher. Let him take your class for a few weeks, and you take his class. It might be a refreshing change for both you and the students!
9. Conduct a "rap session" after school (say once a week), and make it available to any of your students who wish to participate.
10. Try to arrange to bring into your class outside guest speakers to add more reality and variety to your class.
11. Experiment with a contract program. Develop with your students a contract for learning.
12. Let your students be partially involved in planning a course. For example, you could present a long list of subjects to study, problems to investigate, issues for discussion, etc., and then allow the students some freedom to select from this list areas they wish to emphasize.
13. Experiment with alternatives to examinations and tests. Let your students suggest other forms for helping them learn.

14. Question yourself honestly as to why you give tests. Let your students suggest other forms for helping them learn.

15. Have the students make up a test based upon your subject (or subjects) and you take the test. (Dare you to try it!)

16. Experiment with some part of your class time with free time for unstructured activity. Observe how the students use this time; gradually give more free time as both you and your students feel comfortable with it.

17. Take some new courses yourself in areas with which you are unfamiliar. Open up divergent learning responsibilities for yourself.

18. Avoid lecturing for a few days, and confine your teaching style to asking questions, . . . or let students ask you (or other students) questions.

19. Develop open-ended questions with no right answers to encourage divergent thinking.

20. Do something at which you are unskilled and have great difficulty in learning, and something that you find yourself frustrated in doing. (This may help you to empathize more with your students.)

21. Consider the possibility of getting involved in some type of personal growth group. Most college and university extension programs offer some type of week-end group designed for the personal and professional growth of teachers. There are many growth centers that also offer some dynamic programs.

22. You can get an idea of how your students feel about you and your class by providing them with the opportunity to evaluate your program. Below are some samples of the kinds of open-ended questions that could be useful in gaining this kind of feedback. I recommend that these evaluations be anonymous for receiving more honest responses. You can develop specific questions relating to various aspects of your course, the way your students see you, what they feel they are learning, etc. Here are just a few sample questions:

    (a) How does it feel to be a student in this class?
    (b) What do you most like about this class?
    (c) What are some of the things you least like about this class?
    (d) Describe in your own words how you see your teacher. How do you feel toward your teacher?
    (e) How do you feel your teacher sees you as a class?
    (f) What are some things about this class that are different from your other classes?
    (g) What are some things you would most like to change about this class?
    (h) What do you most want to learn from this class?

(i) Do you feel you have the opportunity in this class to discuss your own feelings as a person?

(j) What are some of the most exciting and rewarding things you've done in the class so far?

(k) To what degree do you feel your teacher trusts your class?

(l) What are some characteristics you look for in a teacher? What is your idea of a truly outstanding teacher? What is he like as a person?

(m) What do you most want from your teacher?

(n) What are some things that bother you the most about teachers in general?

(o) Please use the rest of the space to write any comments you have about this class, the teacher, or any observations you care to make.

23. Develop a personalized reading program. Unfortunately, many teachers have an aversion to reading in the field of education. Some thoughtful books have been recently written devoted to ways of changing schools along humanistic lines. Many of these books are found in the annotated reading list which follows. Read through this list and select some readings which catch your eye.

TWENTY QUESTIONS

Below are twenty questions based upon the core themes of this book. I encourage you to give serious thought to these questions BEFORE you read this book, and then reexamine them AFTER completing the book. These questions can be useful for small group discussions within a classroom, for personal reflection, and for general discussions in education courses. Attempt to formulate some of your own questions as you work through the list:

1. Take the title of this book—*Teachers* Can *Make a Difference*—and apply the theme to your own experiences as a learner. How many teachers have you had that *did* make a significant difference in your life? What were they like as persons? How much of them have you incorporated into your own self?

2. Review, reexperience, and attempt to remember as vividly as you can the meaning of your experiences as a learner in elementary school to your present level. What did it feel like to be a student at each level? What did you *really* learn? How did your earlier education either help or hinder you in your present development? What would you most like to change about your own education? If you could relive your entire career as a student, how

would you like it to be different? What were the best experiences you had in school? How about some of the worst experiences?

3. Examine the effects of your own schooling in terms of how it has shaped the kind of teacher you are (or expect to become), and how your schooling has influenced both your philosophy of education and your actual classroom behavior. Are you the conditioned product of your schooling or are you transcending the limitations of your schooling?

4. To what degree were you a teacher-pleaser, and how well did you learn to play academic games? Do you now, as a teacher, demand that your students play these same games? What are some of the games you find yourself playing, and with what results?

5. Were you a self-motivated learner, or did you depend upon teachers to motivate you? If you have learned only when prodded, how can you possibly create a climate where your students can become self-directed learners? If you are a passive learner, how can you expect to help your students become active learners?

6. Do you believe that competition against others is essential for learning to occur? How would the classroom where competition with oneself was stressed be different from the classroom where competition against others was emphasized?

7. To what degree do you search for right answers? Can you accept a diversity of answers, or do you need absolutes? Which is more important to you—the question or the answer? Are you able to tolerate ambiguity or do you need to find certainty?

8. Make a list of all the important things you have learned in school. How many learnings are related to academic subjects? To intellectual areas? To your personal feelings? To life itself? What have you learned inside of the classroom about yourself?

9. What do you see as the main aims of education? What are the functions of the teacher? What should the student be expected to do? How do you feel about having your students evaluate you as a teacher and suggest ways of changing the class?

10. When you reflect upon your own experiences as a learner, ask yourself: How much structure and direction did I need and want? What would have happened had I been encouraged to assume even more responsibility for my own learning? What if there were no requirements, and no grades—what then?

11. Think of the many personal needs that are being met in your work as a teacher. If you are preparing to become a teacher, explore the possible personal needs that might be fulfilled through teaching. Do you need to be needed? Do you enjoy your role as an authority figure? In what ways are you experiencing power as a teacher that you might not otherwise experience? Is teaching a source of emotional, social, and financial security for

you? What are you doing for others as a teacher, and what are you receiving from this giving? What are you *getting* from your students? In what specific ways do they enhance your ego?

12. How much attention have you devoted to your own personal growth as preparation for becoming a teacher? What are some specific ways of growing that you experience? When you are honest with yourself, which direction do you value more: doing what will bring you security or engaging in risky behavior that might bring growth, but which entails leaving the secure?

13. Make an examination of your personal assets and liabilities. What are the specific personal characteristics that you deem crucial for a teacher to acquire? What are some factors within you that you suspect might be barriers to becoming as effective a teacher as possible?

14. From what you have read or already know about personal growth groups or encounter groups, what do you think of this way of growth for yourself? What are your feelings about being a participant in such groups? How do you think classrooms might be different if more teachers were involved in some type of ongoing group where they were encouraged to explore their personal and professional problems relating to their work as teachers? What are some other specific means that you see that teachers can use to keep more open to the possibilities of personal growth and change?

15. Critically evaluate your own teacher training program. How much attention has been given to expanding your own awareness as a person? In your formal teacher preparation, what experiences have you had which were aimed at helping you know yourself more fully and to understand potential effects of your personal dynamics upon students and the learning process?

16. If you could design a teacher education program, what would it look like? What aspects of the program would be given particular emphasis? How would you modify this program from the one you experienced or are now experiencing?

17. Can teachers really make a difference in the lives of the students they teach, or do we delude ourselves into believing we can and must make a difference? Assume that you are able to create a free and open climate where your students are able to blossom as learners. What happens next year if they have a closed teacher? Are most of your effects undone? Are there any long-lasting changes in students? How do you measure or assess these changes? How do you know if you are making a difference or not?

18. After you read chapter 7 (Teachers Who Are Making a Difference), describe the personality characteristics that these four teachers have in common as perceived by their students. From

what you read of each of these four teachers, what do you hear them saying about their role as teachers, their views of students, and their views of what learning is? How do their classrooms seem different from many traditional ones? Based upon what their students wrote, what are the characteristics they value in teachers? What kind of person makes a difference for them?

19. Can real change occur *within* the present educational system? Or is it necessary to destroy the present structure and replace it with a new one? Brainstorm for a time and suggest some features of your ideal school. What changes would you *most* like to see in the present educational system? For every phase of the system you propose discarding, come up with alternatives. Why do you suppose that educators are fearful of changing the schools? Why is change perceived as a threat? What are the barries you see within yourself that make educational change either a slow or non-existent phenomenon? How do you think schools might be different if teachers really believed and acted as though they did have the power to effect significant change?

20. Are you a reader? Do you ever read any books (either in your subject field or in education or psychology) which are not required as textbooks for a course? When you do read books, how do you read them—for grasping what the professor wants or for your own needs? How many books have you read in the past year that relate to teaching and learning? If you find yourself turned off to reading, then how do you expect to get your students turned on to books?

From my work with teachers, I find most of them adverse to reading. With those who are preparing to become teachers, I find many of them are so accustomed to studying textbooks that they merely read what is required and usually for the professor's purposes. Often they claim they feel guilty over the fact they are reading books in education and actually enjoying them. Let me strongly encourage you to examine the annotated reading list which follows. Reading some of these books is one of the best ways of gaining new ideas and of getting some encouragement to begin modifying your classroom procedures. A way of extending the message of this book is by developing your own personalized reading program. Select a few of these titles and see if your interest in reading can be rekindled.

An Annotated Reading List for Teachers:
Key Books in Education and Psychology

One of the best ways to incorporate new ideas into your teaching practices is by developing a personalized reading program. The following books constitute an inexpensive and comprehensive library of humanism for educators. Almost all of these books are available in paperback, and the prices range from one to five dollars. They have been read by teachers and prospective teachers, and have been rated as very useful. If you read about two books from this list each week for your own purposes, you will have completed this list in one year. Begin your reading program now, and learn how to read selectively by taking from each book aspects that seem to have meaning for you.

Books on Criticism of Traditional Education

1. Dennison, George. *The Lives of Children.* New York: Vintage Books, Random House, 1969.
   Dennison makes the children of the First Street School the subject of this classic book in education. It shows what a free and humane education can be like.

2. Farber, Jerry. *The Student as Nigger.* Contact Books.
   Controversial ideas are presented in this book by a controversial English professor, who treats the nature of the master to slave relation in traditional education.

3. Friedenberg, Edgar. *Coming of Age in America.* New York: Vintage Books, Random House, 1965.
   This is a critical review of the secondary school in which the author draws comparisons between schools and prisons. There is some excellent material, but it is a difficult book to read.

4. Goodman, Paul. *Compulsory Mis-Education* and *The Community of Scholars.* New York: Random House, 1966.
   Goodman contends that institutionalized education is inefficient, boring, and damaging to the learner. He argues that teachers must disassociate themselves from institutions and form small nuclear schools.

5. Goodman, Paul. *Growing Up Absurd.* New York: Vintage Books, Random House, 1960.
   This a classic in the field of adolescent psychology deals with some of the key problems of youth in our society.

187

6. Holt, John. *How Children Fail.* New York: Dell, 1964.
   Here is one book every educator should read and think about. Holt explains in clear style why and how children fail in elementary school, and he shows how the school itself is geared toward failure. This an outstanding, easily read work.

7. Holt, John. *How Children Learn.* New York: Dell, 1967.
   This book is excellent for elementary teachers. It deals with games, talking, reading, sports, math, art, etc. Holt takes the position that children are naturally curious and have a built-in will to learn; and that we can *trust* children to learn.

8. Holt, John. *The Underachieving School.* New York: Delta Books, Dell, 1969.
   Holt gives a biting critique of what schools do to learners, along with some proposals for constructive change. Some of the chapter titles are: "Schools are Bad Places for Kids," "Teachers Talk Too Much," "The Tyranny of Testing," "Making Children Hate Reading," and "Education for the Future."

9. Lembo, John. *Why Teachers Fail.* Columbus, Ohio: Charles E. Merrill, 1971.
   Lembo's topics are: Destructive institutional processes, the inquiry process, characteristics of competent teachers, improving the competency of teachers, and conditions of successful school learning.

10. Kirschbaum, Howard, Sidney Simon, and Rodney Napier. *Wad-Ja-Get? The Grading Game in American Education.* New York: Hart, 1971.
    This work is a discussion of the grading system and its effects upon students. The possible alternatives to the grading system are examined.

11. Rasberry, Salli and Robert Greenway. *The Rasberry Exercises: How to Start Your Own School and Make a Book.* Freestone, Calif.: Freestone Publishing, 1970.
    A unique book! It shows the limitations of traditional education and describes ways and means of creating alternative schools and free schools. This very good work includes a bibliography and sources to write for further ideas.

12. Silberman, Charles. *Crisis in the Classroom.* New York: Vintage Books, Random House, 1970.
    This already-classic work points to some of the major ills of traditional education and suggests a direction for reform.

On Ways of Changing Education

13. Glasser, William. *Schools Without Failure.* New York: Harper & Row, 1969.
    This contemporary book is being widely used in elementary schools to effect change of traditional patterns. Glasser deals with failure and its effects, the problems of conventional education, ways of implementing new programs, and guides for class meetings.

14. Leonard, George. *Education and Ecstasy.* New York: Delta Books, Dell, 1968.

A "must" for every educator! The book analyses the limitations of the traditional school and calls for a school which maximizes human potential. A utopian view of education is presented. The theme of this very interesting and readable book is that learning should be a joy.

15. Postman, Neil and Charles Weingartner. *Teaching as a Subversive Activity.* New York: Delta Books, Dell, 1969.
    Here is a book that is worth being on the library shelf of every teacher. Its theme is that teachers ought to teach students how to think critically. This book is filled with thought-provoking ideas and with concrete suggestions as to how teachers can make some changes within the walls of their classes.

16. Postman, Neil and Charles Weingartner. *The Soft Revolution.* New York: Delta Books, Dell, 1971.
    This student handbook advocates a nonviolent revolution whereby high school and college students can use the present educational system to change the system drastically. It makes very interesting reading.

17. Renfield, Richard. *If Teachers Were Free.* New York: Delta Books, Dell, 1969.
    What would a teacher's task be like if he saw his task as *helping* learning to happen rather than *making* it happen? What would happen if children were free to question all things? This book deals with these issues.

18. Torrance, Paul. *Encouraging Creativity in the Classroom.* Dubuque, Iowa: William C. Brown, 1970.
    The author's intent is to encourage the teacher to come to awareness of the possibilities of his own creativity. Areas discussed are the relationship of creativity to learning, responding to creative needs, encountering the unexpected, going beyond textbooks, and awakening hidden potential.

Humanistic Education: Alternatives to Conventional Education

19. Borton, Terry. *Reach, Touch, and Teach.* New York: McGraw-Hill, 1970.
    This is a beautiful book that deals with student concerns and process education. It also deals with reaching and touching students as individual human beings, and demonstrates how "new ways" of teaching can occur. This excellent book is rich with resources and ideas for elementary or secondary teachers who want to learn more about humanistic education.

20. Brown, George. *Human Teaching For Human Learning.* New York: Viking, 1971.
    This excellent current book provides an introduction to confluent education. Brown describes a variety of effective techniques that can be used to bring together the intellectual and emotional aspects of learning. He gives examples of how humanistic education has worked for elementary and secondary teachers.

21. Clark, Donald and Asya Kadis. *Humanistic Teaching.* Columbus, Ohio: Charles E. Merrill, 1971.

This work deals with a group approach to classroom living and discusses examples of behavior problems in the classroom, including ways of coping with specific problems. The authors suggest human solutions for common problems in the classroom.

22. Davis, David. *Model for a Humanistic Education: The Danish Folk Highschool.* Columbus, Ohio: Charles E. Merrill, 1971.
    This book gives an example of how schools can be designed to facilitate human learning. It includes an excellent annotated bibliography.

23. Dillon, J. T. *Personal Teaching.* Columbus, Ohio: Charles E. Merrill, 1971.
    This book will be of interest to the high school teacher who wishes to move from a traditional to a more freeing type of classroom. The author describes his methods of teaching and shares his own struggles in moving to a student-centered classroom. The book contains student reactions to his program.

24. Greer, Mary and Bonnie Rubenstein. *Will the Real Teacher Please Stand Up?* Pacific Palisades, Calif.: Goodyear Publishing, 1972.
    This is a different book containing a wide variety of short readings in humanistic education, games that can be used in classrooms, suggestions for exploring ideas and feelings in classes, and activities that can be implemented.

25. Jones, Richard. *Fantasy and Feeling in Education.* New York: Harper & Row, 1968.
    The author calls for a wedding of psychotherapy and education. He contends that we must discover how to involve the child's emotions and imagination. The book is based on his experimental social studies curriculum: "Man—a course of study."

26. Kline, Lloyd. *Education and the Personal Quest.* Columbus, Ohio: Charles E. Merrill, 1971.
    Kline examines the origin of change in schools, the goals of education, and some alternatives to the present system.

27. Lederman, Janet. *Anger and the Rocking Chair.* New York: McGraw-Hill, 1969.
    This is an account of Gestalt awareness methods used in a classroom of "difficult" children. Lederman shows how children can become aware of their feelings and their power as a person.

28. Lyon, Harold. *Learning to Feel—Feeling to Learn.* Columbus, Ohio: Charles E. Merrill, 1971.
    Lyon deals with the problem of the intellectual half-man and provides guidelines for humanizing education. Chapters 4 and 5 are excellent for sources of humanistic techniques which can be applied to classroom situations. The book has an excellent bibliography on humanistic education.

29. Perls, Frederick. *Gestalt Therapy Verbatim.* Moab, Utah: Real People Press, 1969.

This work contains excellent sources of various affective techniques based upon Gestalt therapy exercises.

30. Perls, Frederick, Ralph Hefferline, and Paul Goodman. *Gestalt Therapy: Excitement and Growth in the Human Personality.* New York: Dell, 1951.
   The authors present the theoretical as well as the applied aspects of Gestalt therapy. In a series of eighteen experiments, the reader is an active participant in the growth of self-discovery.

31. Rogers, Carl. *Freedom to Learn.* Columbus, Ohio: Charles E. Merrill, 1969.
   Here is a view of what education might become. This book calls for freedom instead of a stifling authoritarian approach to education. Methods of creating this climate of freedom are discussed. This is a must for anyone in teaching.

The Summerhill Approach to Education

32. Bull, Richard. *Summerhill, U.S.A.* Baltimore: Penguin, 1970.
   This is a picture survey of the free-school concept and how it works in the United States. It provides a look at the daily life of American free schools. Staff members and students describe how they live, compare the Summerhill way with more traditional learning ways, tell what they hope to gain from their education, and talk about the experiences of students who have left.

33. Hart, Harold, ed. *Summerhill: For and Against.* New York: Hart, 1970.
   Writers in education, psychology, and sociology evaluate A. S. Neill's Summerhill School. Some of the writers include Max Rafferty, Paul Goodman, Erich Fromm, John Holt, Goodwin Watson, and Bruno Bettelheim.

34. Neill, A. S. *Freedom — Not License!* New York: Hart, 1966.
   This is a follow-up on Summerhill. Neill answers the questions of American parents in areas such as anti-life attitudes, school, sex, influencing children, problems of children and adolescents, family tensions, and therapy.

35. Neill, A. S. *Summerhill: A Radical Approach to Child Rearing.* New York: Hart, 1964.
   Here is a book that you cannot read passively. It is an easy-to-read, but challenging and stimulating work that deals with the free school, child rearing, sex education, religion, and other aspects of child development. It is a must for anyone dealing with children.

36. Popenoe, Joshua. *Inside Summerhill.* New York: Hart, 1970.
   The experience of Summerhill School in England is told by a 16-year-old boy who spent four years at Summerhill. He gives a good "feel" of the atmosphere—along with many photographs.

37. Snitzer, Herb. *Living at Summerhill.* New York: P. F. Collier, 1964.
   This is a picture documentary of A. S. Neill's school which deals with the highlights of *Summerhill.*

38. Walmsley, John. *Neill and Summerhill: A Man and His Work*. Baltimore: Penguin, 1969.
    This is another pictorial study of Neill's Summerhill. Students and teachers at Summerhill give their impressions of the school.

Books about Teachers Who Have Changed their Classrooms

39. Ashton-Warner, Sylvia. *Teacher*. New York: Bantam Books, 1963.
    This is an account by a teacher who knows the meaning of love, joy, and care. It is a well known book that could inspire other teachers.

40. Decker, Sunny. *An Empty Spoon*. New York: Perennial Library, Harper & Row, 1969.
    This book is the account of a new teacher's first two years in a ghetto school.

41. Hentoff, Nat. *Our Children are Dying*. New York: Viking, 1966.
    This is the story of how Dr. Elliot Shapiro, principal of Harlem School, met the problems posed, and how he crusaded for new forms of education.

42. Herndon, James. *The Way It Spozed To Be*. New York: Bantam Books, 1969.
    This is an interesting account of one man's encounter as a first-year teacher. Read this if you want to find out what happened when he attempted to rebel against the authoritarian structure and give his students more freedom.

43. Joseph, Stephen M., ed. *The Me Nobody Knows*. New York: Avon Books, 1969.
    This anthology is based upon the open writings of children in ghettos. The book shows ways of relating writing to the lives of the students. It is easy and quick reading, but says a lot! Joseph includes excellent resource ideas.

44. Kaufman, Bell. *Up the Down Staircase*. New York: Avon Books, 1964.
    Funny, true, interesting! This best-seller depicts the experiences of a young teacher in a metropolitan high school.

45. Kohl, Herbert. *The Open Classroom*. New York: Vintage Books, Random House, 1969.
    This is an easy-reading, practical, interesting, and stimulating handbook for teachers who wish to learn how to develop an open and free classroom. Kohl presents ideas and strategies for experimentation. It is an honest book, written in direct style, and is most helpful.

46. Kohl, Herbert. *36 Children*. New York: Signet Books, New American Library, 1967.
    This is a touching, honest, and inspirational account of a young teacher's year in a ghetto classroom. Kohl is an example of an authentic person who dares to show his humanness to his students. This is one book that every teacher ought to read.

47. Kozol, Jonathan. *Death at an Early Age.* New York: Bantam Books, 1967. This honest, interesting, dymanic account shows what it is like to be a student and a teacher in an American ghetto school. It is a powerful book that shows how the minds and hearts of Negro children are destroyed in a ghetto school.

48. Mirthes, Caroline. *Can't You Hear Me Talking To You?* New York: Bantam Books, 1971. This fascinating book is written by school children in the ghetto. It shows a way to introduce both a reading and writing program in your classroom.

49. Summers, Andrew. *Me the Flunkie.* New York: Fawcett Work Library, 1970. In this book the work of school failures is presented. It is useful in getting the feel of what the world of the school failure is like.

Books on Dynamics of Teacher's Personal Feelings

50. Boy, Angelo and Gerald Pine. *Expanding the Self: Personal Growth for Teachers.* Dubuque, Iowa: William C. Brown, 1971. The authors deal with the personhood of the teacher. The theme of the book is that when students learn, it is because they respond to the teacher as a person. The human, vocational, religious, and recreational aspects of the personhood of the teacher are explored with implications for teaching.

51. Greenberg, Herbert. *Teaching With Feeling.* Indianapolis: Pegasus, Bobbs-Merrill, 1969. The intellecutal aspects of education are often stressed to the exclusion of human emotions and feelings. Here is a book that treats the importance of the emotional aspects of learning.

52. Jersild, Arthur. *When Teachers Face Themselves.* New York: Teachers College, 1955. This is a good introduction to the theme of the importance of each teacher learning how to accept and deal with anxiety, loneliness, meaning in life, sex, hostility, and compassion.

53. Moustakas, Clark. *The Authentic Teacher.* Cambridge, Mass.: Howard A. Doyle, 1966. Moustakas provides a basis for genuine committment to the interpersonal process in learning. He suggests ways in which the teacher can bring his own unique self to the classroom and facilitate growth in himself and children. Topics treated include authenticity and betrayal, creating a real relationship, mental health approaches in elementary grades, and self-exploration among high school students.

54. Natalicio, Luiz and Carl Hereford. *The Teacher as a Person.* Dubuque, Iowa: William C. Brown, 1971. This book includes ten provocative readings exploring such themes as self-acceptance, what it means to become a person, the place of affective

learning, significant learning in therapy and education, confrontation and encounter, and why teachers fail.

Books Dealing with Personal Growth

55. Feifel, Herman, ed. *The Meaning of Death.* New York: McGraw-Hill, 1959.
    This is an excellent selection of essays on death. Some topics are the soul and death, the fear of death, a child's view of death, existentialism and death, modern art and death, the doctor and death, death and religion, suicide and death. This book contains eighteen separate articles, each written by a different authority.

56. Frankl, Victor. *Doctor and Soul.* New York: Bantam Books, 1965.
    This book explains the theory of logotherapy, an existential form of life, and an approach to therapy.

57. Frankl, Victor. *Man's Search for Meaning.* New York: Washington Square Press, 1959.
    The author describes his experiences in a German concentration camp and shows how it is possible to find a meaning in life through suffering. Frankl's theme is "He who has a *why* for living can bear with almost any *how!*" Frankl feels that man's supreme motive is a searching for personal meaning. You probably will not be able to put this book down until you finish.

58. Fromm, Erich. *The Art of Loving.* New York: Bantam Books, 1956.
    Love in all its aspects is the subject of this book. The book is a philosophy of love, and it is the kind of book that you can read many times with deeper insights upon each reading.

59. Greene, Maxine, ed. *Existential Encounters for Teachers.* New York: Random House, 1967.
    Samples of the writings of key existential thinkers form the essence of the book. Authors include Kierkegaard, Heidegger, Sartre, Jaspers, Buber, Camus, Marcel, Nietzsche, Kafka, Dostoevsky, and Tillich. The selections have implications for teachers and education.

60 Hodge, Marshall. *Your Fear of Love.* New York: Doubleday, 1967.
    This very useful and easy-to-read book explains how our fears originate and how they prevent us from loving. Some topics include our fears of freedom, anger, sex, manhood, and womanhood. Hodge discusses some guides to learning how to live for ourselves.

61. Jourard, Sidney. *Disclosing Man to Himself.* New York: D. Van Nostrand, 1968.
    This is an excellent example of the humanistic approach to psychology. The orientation is toward psychotherapy for growth. Application of psychotherapy to learning is made.

62. Jourard, S. M. *The Transparent Self,* rev. ed. New York: D. Van Nostrand, 1971.

The author holds that we have many ways of concealing our real self, instead of being open. He maintains that our lack of openness results in sickness, maladjustment, and alienation from ourselves.

63. Knoblock, Peter and Arnold Goldstein. *The Lonely Teacher*. Boston: Allyn & Bacon, 1971.
   This book describes an encounter group experience for teachers with a discussion of the problems dealt with and the outcomes of the group process.

64. Kubler-Ross, Elizabeth. *On Death and Dying*. New York: Macmillan, 1969.
   This is a thoughtful treatment of the fear of death and attitudes toward death and dying. The book was formed from interviews with terminal cancer patients.

65. Lyon, William. *Let Me Live!* North Quincy, Mass.: Christopher Publishing, 1970.
   Are you getting what you deserve from life? Why not? This book was written by a practicing clinical psychologist and is designed to show the reader how to assess his own problem areas, develop a better self-concept, and achieve his goals. It deals frankly and interestingly with areas such as seeing the world as it is; self-evaluation; love, sex, marriage; therapy groups; and finding a meaning in life. This is a very useful book for personal growth.

66. Marshall, Bernice, ed. *Experiences in Being*. Belmont, Calif.: Brooks/Cole Publishing, Wadsworth, 1971.
   A different book with an exciting format. Deals with emerging images of man as man, man as himself, man with others, and man and his constructions.

67. Maslow, Abraham. *Motivation and Personality*, 2nd ed. New York: Harper & Row, 1970.
   This is one of Maslow's major works; it describes a psychology of persons based upon health and self-actualization.

68. Maslow, Abraham. *Toward a Psychology of Being*, 2nd ed. New York: D. Van Nostrand, 1968.
   This book is Maslow's second major work. It deals with growth and motivation, creativity, values, and the self-actualizing person. It contains good material, but is not easy reading. The ideas here are helpful for educators.

69. May, Rollo, ed. *Existential Psychology*, 2nd ed. New York: Random House, 1969.
   Key authors such as Rollo May, Gordon Allport, Herman Feifel, Abraham Maslow, and Carl Rogers have contributed separate articles describing their views of existential psychology. If you are interested in the existential view of man, this book is an excellent starting place.

70. May, Rollo. *Man's Search for Himself*. New York: Signet Books, New American Library, 1953.

This is a very thought-provoking book for those interested in soul searching and expanding self-knowledge. May deals with loneliness, anxiety, the predicament of modern man, the experiences of becoming a person, struggling to be, freedom, maturity, religion, and goals for living. This outstanding work can be reread many times with new insight.

71. Moustakas, Clark E. *Creativity and Conformity*. New York: D. Van Nostrand Company, 1967.
    This book takes a stand in behalf of individuality and creativity. The consequences of conformity in our age are discussed. This work is not a single essay, but a series of papers which treat topics such as creativity and conformity, individuality and uniqueness, man's relationship to man, ethical values, and man's search for truth and meaning.

72. Moustakas, Clark. *Loneliness*. Englewood Cliffs, N.J.: Spectrum Books, Prentice-Hall, 1961.
    The central message of this book is that loneliness is a condition of human life; and without the experience of loneliness we cannot find ourselves. Through loneliness we can extend and deepen our humanity. Several cases of loneliness are presented, each helping to develop the concept of the necessity of loneliness.

73. Moustakas, Clark. *Loneliness and Love*. Englewood Cliffs, N.J.: Spectrum Books, Prentice-Hall, 1972.
    This book offers a unique approach to the positive dimensions of loneliness, emphasizing individuality, personal honesty, communication, love, and their relation to one's self.

74. Perls, Frederick. *In and Out of the Garbage Pail*. Moab, Utah: Real People Press, 1969.
    This is a novel autobiography in which Perls applies his theory of focusing on awareness. Partly in poetic form, often playful, sometimes theoretical, the book is a many-faceted mosaic of memories and reflection of his life—in the past and at the moment—and on the origins and continuing development of Gestalt therapy.

75. Rogers, Carl. *On Becoming a Person*. Boston: Sentry Editions, Houghton-Mifflin, 1961.
    This is a compilation of many of Carl Rogers' significant essays on education, therapy, communication, family life, and the healthy person. It is an outstanding work that should be on the shelf of every educator.

76. Rogers, Carl R. and Barry Stevens, eds. *Person to Person: The Problem of Being Human: A New Trend in Psychology*. Moab, Utah: Real People Press, 1967.
    Although this paperback brings together previously published papers by Rogers, Gendlin, and Van Dusen, it is quite unlike the typical edited compilation. This very unconventional book makes for interesting and stimulating reading.

77. Shostrom, Everett. *Man the Manipulator*. New York: Bantam Books, 1967.
    This easy-reading, popular book discusses the differences between

manipulators and actualizors. Various examples of styles of manipulation are given. The goals of actualization are given, and the process of growing from manipulation to actualization is discussed.

78. Stevens, Barry. *Don't Push the River*. Moab, Utah: Real People Press, 1969.
This is a first person account of the author's use of Gestalt therapy and the ways of Zen, Krishnamurti, and the American Indian to deepen and expand personal experiences and work through difficulties. "We have to turn ourselves upside down and reverse our approach to life."

Books on Encounter Groups

79. Blank, Leonard, Gloria Gottsegan, and Monroe Gottsegan, eds. *Confrontation: Encounter in Self and Interpersonal Awareness*. New York; Macmillan, 1971.
This is a book of readings dealing with the experience of encounter. It deals with process of marathons, techniques and various approaches, innovations in group work, applications to education, business and industry, and theory and research. The editors provide comprehensive coverage in the twenty-two separate readings.

80. Egan, Gerard. *Encounter Groups: Basic Readings*. Belmont Calif.: Brooks/Cole Publishing, Wadsworth, 1971.
This is a book of readings on goals, leadership, self-disclosure, support, confrontation, research and other phases of encounter groups.

81. Egan, Gerard. *Encounter: Group Processes for Interpersonal Growth*. Belmont, Calif.: Brooks/Cole Publishing, Wadsworth, 1970.
This book is a thorough, excellent treatment (with numerous references) on the nature of encounter groups. Egan deals with group goals, group process, leadership, self-disclosure, and personal growth.

82. Gunther, Bernard. *Sense Relaxation*. New York: P. F. Collier, 1968.
Gunther deals with the forgotten language of touch and feeling. Many of the nonverbal techniques used at Esalen Institute in Big Sur are described.

83. Mahler, Clarence. *Group Counseling in the Schools*. Boston: Houghton-Mifflin, 1969.
This is one of the best books on the nature, process, and outcomes of group counseling in secondary schools. It is well-written and easy-reading.

84. Miles, Matthew. *Learning to Work in Groups*. New York: Teachers College Press, 1959.
This practical guide and handbook on group work for teachers contains specific instructions and a good bibliography.

85. Moustakas, Clark. *Individuality and Encounter*. Cambridge, Mass.: Howard A. Doyle, 1968.
Chapter 4 of this book deals with an account of an encounter group in which the author relates his own experiences. He discusses his own thoughts on groups, approaches and techniques, etc. Other themes treated

are individuality and encounter, loneliness and solitude, and loneliness and encounter. This is excellent reading and highly recommended for people in encounter groups.

86. Moustakas, Clark. *Personal Growth: The Struggle for Identity and Human Values.* Cambridge, Mass.: Howard A. Doyle, 1969.
This book is excellent reading for personal growth groups consisting of teachers. Moustakas writes clearly and opens thoughts up on such issues as alienation and education, creativity and conformity in education, the authentic self, and authentic versus inauthentic learning.

87. Otto, H. A. and John Mann. *Ways of Growth: Approaches to Expanding Awareness.* New York: Viking, 1968.
This series of nineteen separate articles on ways of growth includes essays on growing self-awareness, breathing therapy, sensory awakening and relaxation, sex and awareness, the encounter group, peak experiences, meditation, leaderless groups, and the psychedelic experience.

88. Rogers, Carl. *Carl Rogers on Encounter Groups.* New York: Harper & Row, 1970.
This is an excellent introduction to what encounter groups are about. Rogers deals with the process and outcomes of encounter groups, change as a result of these groups, and the person's experience in groups.

89. Schutz, William. *Joy: Expanding Human Awareness.* New York: Grove Press, 1967.
The theme of this book is that joy is the result of our realizing our full human potentialities. Methods of enhancing our personal functioning and our interpersonal relationships make up the core of the book. Schutz deals with encounter group methods used at marathon-type workshops to help people expand awareness of the range of their human potentials.

Books on Child and Adolescent Development

90. Axline, Virginia. *Dibs: In Search of Self.* New York: Ballantine Books, 1964.
This is a touching book about a boy's journey to self-awareness. It is the kind of book that you find hard to put aside until you've finished.

91. Axline, Virginia. *Play Therapy.* New York: Ballantine Books.
This work deals with the dynamics and process of play therapy. It is a good follow-up to *Dibs.*

92. Baruch, Dorothy. *One Little Boy.* New York: Delta Books, Dell, 1964.
This is an outstanding account of one boy's feelings and problems as revealed through play therapy. The book gives the reader a real feeling of problems faced by all children through the therapy of Kenneth.

93. Bettelheim, Bruno. *Love is Not Enough.* New York: P. F. Collier, 1950.
This is about the treatment of emotionally distrubed children at the special school for the seriously disturbed. It shows how these children are taught to trust people.

94. Bettelheim, Bruno. *Truants from Life: The Rehabilitation of Emotionally Disturbed Children.* New York: Free Press, Macmillan, 1955.
   This is a follow-up book to *Love is Not Enough.* In this excellent book, four in-depth case studies are presented, illustrating how seriously disturbed children gradually come to discover themselves and their real feelings. The cases of Paul, Mary, John, and Harry show how children learn how to trust, love, and enter into life. The background factors causing the disorders of each child are well presented.

95. Ginott, Haim. *Between Parent and Child.* New York: Avon Books, 1969.
   This is a good, easy-to-read book for the layman. Its purpose is to show how to listen to what children are really saying. It treats a variety of timely issues in child rearing.

96. Ginott, Haim. *Between Parent and Teen-Ager.* New York: Avon Books, 1969.
   This is an easy-to-read book treating rebellion, anger, praise, social life, sex, values, drugs, and a philosophy of parent–adolescent relations.

97. Golburgh, Stephen, ed. *The Experience of Adolescence.* Cambridge, Mass.: Schenkman Publishing, Inc., 1965.
   The material in this book is designed to produce a *feeling* for the experience of adolescence. The book contains twenty-five "personal documents" of various adolescent experiences, as told by adolescents. It is an excellent book for students of adolescent psychology.

98. Green, Hannah. *I Never Promised You a Rose Garden.* New York: Signet Books, New American Library, 1964.
   This is a story of a sixteen-year-old schizophrenic girl which illustrates her retreat from reality and flight into her imaginary world. The book does a good job of showing the reader the inner world of a psychotic.

99. Moustakas, Clark. *Psychotherapy With Children.* New York: Ballantine Books, 1959.
   In this book Moustakas deals with play therapy and other modes of therapy with children. It is helpful if you want further ways of working with children therapeutically.

100. Ostrovsky, Everett. *Children Without Men.* New York: P. F. Collier, 1966.
   What happens to a child when the father is absent from the home? This is the theme of this work. It includes excellent case studies of preschool children.

ABOUT THE AUTHOR

Gerald F. Corey is currently an Associate Professor of Inter-disciplinary and Special Studies at California State University, Fuller-ton. He received his doctorate in counseling psychology from the University of Southern California in 1967. Dr. Corey is also a licensed psychologist in part-time private practice. He has been involved in teacher education and counselor education, in college counseling, and in college and high school teaching.

Other Publications in the Merrill Studies of the Person Series

Freedom to Learn
Carl R. Rogers

Learning to Feel — Feeling to Learn
Harold C. Lyon, Jr.

Humanistic Teaching
Donald Clark and Asya Kadis

Personal Teaching
J. T. Dillon

Risk–Trust–Love: Learning in a
 Humane Environment
William Romey

Goals and Behavior in Psychotherapy and
 Counseling: Readings and Questions
Jack Huber and Howard Millman

The Learning Community:
 A Humanistic Cookbook for Teachers
Harry Morgan

The Onion Sandwich Principle and
 Other Essays on Classroom Management
Judith Beal Beatty

CHARLES E. MERRILL PUBLISHING COMPANY

A *Bell & Howell* Company   Columbus, Ohio

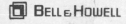 BELL & HOWELL